The Quest for
the Secret Nile

To the memory of my mother, Myrtle Yeoman,
to whom, I know, my father would have wanted this book to be dedicated.

P Y

The Quest for the Secret Nile

Victorian Exploration in Equatorial Africa 1857-1900

Guy Yeoman

CHAUCER PRESS
LONDON

Published by Chaucer Press
20 Bloomsbury Street
London WC1B 3JH

A CIP catalogue record for this book is available from the British Library

ISBN 1-904449-15-8

Designed and produced for Chaucer Press
by Savitri Books Ltd
25 Lisle Lane
Ely CB7 4AS

Reproduced by H K Scanner Arts International Ltd, Hong Kong
Printed by D 2 Print Pte Ltd, Singapore

Endpapers: *Hippopotamuses on the banks of the Semliki River*
Frontispiece illustration: *Looking downstream from the Murchison Falls,
towards Lake Albert*
Pages 6-7: *The sun setting behind an acacia tree, so evocative of Africa*

The portrait of Sir Richard Francis Burton by Frederic Leighton is reproduced by
Courtesy of the National Portrait Gallery, London

Note on Bibliography, see page 186. Guy Yeoman died in 1998 before he had a chance of
completing the present book's bibliography. Sadly, it has proved impossible to trace the entire
and vast reading list on which he drew for this work. The editor apologizes to the readers for
any inconvenience caused by possible inaccuracies or omissions; as well as to the authors,
unknown to us, whose scholarship Guy Yeoman relied on and valued,
but who may have been left out.

Sincere thanks are due to the following individuals: Janine Mellors for assistance
with the preparation of the manuscript; Keith Bullock, Lyndon Cochrane
and Keith Streb for assistance with cartography.

Contents

Foreword

The manuscript for this book was at a late stage
of completion, when my father died suddenly,
on the 3rd of August 1998. To me fell the daunting
task of collating and editing the text, preparing
maps from his sketches and selecting suitable
photographs and illustrations from his extensive
archives. It took me on an evocative journey
through the land of my birth and to the many
beautiful places we visited as a family, when
my father was working as a veterinary surgeon
in Africa, during the 1950s and early 60s. The book
tells an exciting story, often dramatic, sometimes
romantic, set amongst some of the continent's most
spectacular landscapes – the very crucible of Africa.
It is a meeting of history and geography that
is virtually unknown to modern readers.

My father's love affair with East Africa and
its people began in 1942 when, as a young officer,
he was involved in recruiting and training African
troops for the war in Burma.

He became fluent in Swahili and trained as a court interpreter. Through his work,
he developed a detailed understanding of the different cultures of the people of the region.
His travels took him to the Nile, to Lake Victoria and to Lake Albert, where he saw
the great snowy peaks of the Rwenzori mountains for the first time – the Mountains
of the Moon mentioned by the ancient Greeks.

In 1944 his regiment embarked for Burma, but on 12th February a disaster struck that
would leave him with a deep sense of debt to the African people for the rest of his life.
The troopship, *Khedive Ismail*, was torpedoed by a Japanese submarine, while on passage
from Mombasa to Sri Lanka, the old Ceylon. The 1,511 casualties included almost
the entire contingent of African troops of his own regiment, boys who had come from
small villages in the bush and were on their way to fight somebody else's war.

After the war my father completed his veterinary studies, joined the Colonial Office and
was sent to Tanzania, where he carried out field research into cattle diseases, particularly
East Coast fever, which periodically decimated the cattle population of the region, causing
poverty and starvation. The introduction of disease control schemes led to an increase
of the cattle and, consequently, of the human population. Ironically, this development

caused overgrazing and renewed cycles of poverty. Through these early observations, my father came to understand the complexity of the interaction between economics, ecology, geography, culture and sociology. In later years he witnessed many grand schemes designed to bring 'progress' and provide aid to Africa and realised that the efforts of outside agencies, however well meaning, may cause more harm than good in the long run.

Before European explorers penetrated the part of Africa examined in this book – a huge network of lakes, rivers, swamps, mountains, forests and vast savannah plains forming the Nile's headwater complex – it was home to many separate kingdoms and cultures. This secret land remained hidden from the outside world until relatively recent times and, as a result, it maintained a relative prosperity in spite of the ravages caused by the Arab slave trade that brought economic and social upheavals to the coastal and therefore more accessible areas. There was an ecological balance ensuring a constant source of water for the Nile and a political balance of power which kept up a relative stability and protected the population against starvation. In more recent times, much of this region has suffered – and goes on suffering – protracted wars, genocide, ecological depredations, great poverty and starvation. It is this troubled region that also harbours the main sources of the Nile.

Powerful rivers usually have several sources, but most have an *ultimate* source that is both higher than any other and furthest from their mouth. The Nile has several such sources, depending on your definition. The snows of Mount Stanley, in the Rwenzori range, certainly constitute the highest source at over 5,000 m (16.000 ft), but the most southerly headwaters of the Kagera River, in Burundi, are probably the furthest from the Nile's estuary. Each of the thousands of sources, however seemingly insignificant, makes its own contribution to the perennial flow of this majestic river. They now find themselves under threat, be it from global climate change, or from local deforestation and swamp drainage. At least, unlike many of the world's other great rivers, industrial pollution is not yet a significant problem, though this may be only a matter of time.

In the later years of his life my father visited many of these secret sources, situated in remote regions, and captured their outstanding natural beauty on camera. He realised that, without adequate protection for these sources, there was a real possibility that the mighty Nile could simply dry up. There is a widespread belief that, in a world where water may become more important than oil, Africa will be the continent and the Nile the river of this new century. It was my father's hope that his account of the discovery of the Nile sources would capture the interest of the present generation and play its part in making a case for the protection of the unique landscape on which the Nile depends for its survival. Paddy Yeoman, August 2003

Opposite: My father, Guy Yeoman, camped at 3,962 m (13,000 ft) on the west face of the Portal Range of Rwenzori and surrounded by high-altitude giant groundsels.

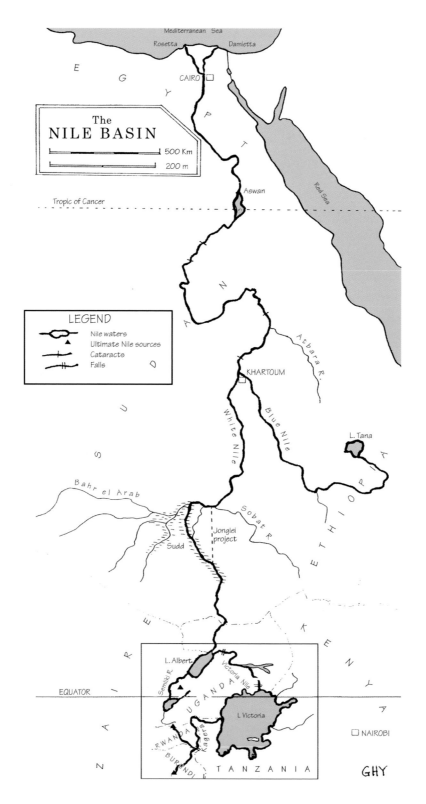

Above: The course of the Nile, as we know it to run today. The section contained inside the box is the region dealt with by the book. A more detailed map of this area appears on the opposite page.

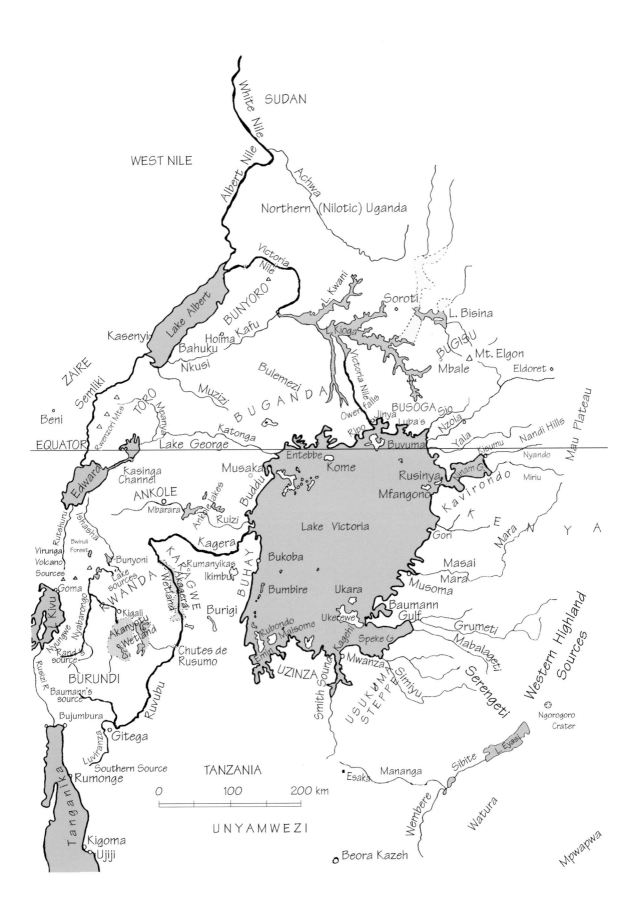

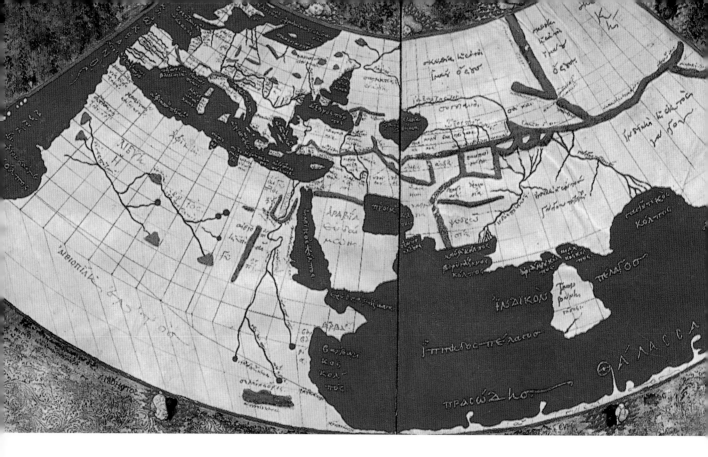

Introduction

The Nile, stretching for a distance of 6,741 km (4,187 miles), is the longest river in the world – a river which represents the cradle of a civilization whose monuments still dominate the landscape of Egypt today. For centuries, the Nile was also the world's great geographic enigma: what was the provenance of so much water, feeding a river that flowed constantly out of the desert? How many Niles were there? The Egyptian Nile was one thing, but what of the mysterious western Nile, supposed to flow into the Gulf of Guinea, having meandered its way across the whole of Africa and whose sources reputedly started in the mythical Mountains of Moon? This riddle had obsessed the ancient Greeks. Aeschylus, in 500 BC, talked of Egypt being nurtured by the snows. A little later, Herodotus actually followed the course of the Nile, upstream, for several hundreds of miles and quoted a story he had heard about the Nile rising from two great equatorial lakes – the *Nili Paludes* – fed by waters from two snow-capped mountains – the *Lunae Montes* – the fabled Mountains of the Moon. In the second century AD the astronomer, mathematician and geographer, Claudius Ptolemy, never stirred from his library in Alexandria, yet, like a sponge, he absorbed all the travellers' tales and, in his book, he writes of a Greek traveller, Diogenes, who had made a journey to the hinterland from the Indian Ocean coast. These tantalizing references to lakes and mountains no one had actually seen in modern times – were they myths or reality? – were nevertheless enough to spur men on to risk their lives in the search for the ultimate sources of the Nile. In the course of the centuries, Roman legionaries, Portuguese Jesuits, adventurous Scots and erudite Frenchmen all tried to solve the riddle, only to be defeated by the terrain or lured along a wrong branch of the headwaters. The enigma would remain unsolved until the mid-nineteenth century.

Victorian Britain was far from immune to this fever of exploration. Away from the turbulent mid-nineteenth-century crises of the Indian Mutiny and of the Crimean War, the Nile headwaters offered young men fresh opportunities for challenge and self-fulfilment. These would-be explorers emerged from the manor houses of the minor

Opposite page, top picture: The world, as seen by Claudius Ptolemy in a map drawn in the twelfth or thirteenth century. The course of the Nile is outlined fairly precisely in the north, but it becomes more tentative in the south. To the left can be seen the basin of the imaginary western Nile. This mixture of part information, part fanciful imaginings would be perpetuated through the centuries.
Bottom picture: This map was drawn in the thirteenth century and illustrates the work of the Arab geographer al-Idrisi. South is at the top of the map which shows the White Nile and the Blue Nile, streaming down the Mountains of the Moon, with one of the rivers flowing into the Atlantic Ocean.

gentry and the hunting fields of rural shires – often via service in the Indian Army – from quiet English vicarages and Scottish manses or from the northern powerhouses of industry, often spurred on by the philanthropy of the wealthy men who were the product of this great industrial expansion. This disparate and ephemeral cast of actors flitted across a savage scene, often to their early and unrecorded deaths, with an almost complete absence of either political or economic motivation. If there was an underlying continuum, it was to be found in a national predilection for adventure and an insatiable sense of curiosity.

The land of the Nile basin was virtually valueless, offering few tangible rewards to foreign investors or prospectors, beyond the immutable burden of fever and, in any case, its situation at the heart of the continent made it difficult to exploit. In the words of Joseph Conrad, any western intrusion was redeemable 'only by the idea...not a sentimental pretence, but an idea; and an unselfish belief in the idea.' This idea – based on the premise that western culture somehow had a duty to aspire and the ability to bring about the uplift of a presumedly static and somehow inferior culture – was reinforced by an intuitive arrogance which made it intolerable that any nation, but Britain, should rule over the ultimate sources of the Nile.

In the later half of the Victorian era, the Nile basin region – in modern terms: southern Uganda, western Kenya, north-western Tanzania, Rwanda, Burundi and extreme eastern Zaire (Congo) – was in the process of being subsumed by contacts with western culture. It had a peculiarly dramatic and romantic history, providing as it did, several diverse interfaces: not only was it the stage for the impact of perceived western enlightenment, versus indigenous savagery and Arab slavery, of Christianity versus Islam, of ascetic Scottish Presbyterianism versus marihuana-soaked sexual hedonism, of Roman Catholicism versus Anglican Protestantism, but also of Germany and France versus Britain.

Western scholars had long known that the dry-season flow of the Egyptian Nile – as opposed to the annual flood by the Blue Nile of Ethiopia – came from Africa's equatoria by means of a giant tributary-less drain – the so-called White Nile. The history and geography of this river were to be widely described by nineteenth-century travellers and writers, but the then universal acceptance of the Ripon Falls as the definitive source of the Nile tended to obscure the fact that for many hundreds of miles to the south, a headwater complex existed – a marvel of lakes, rivers, swamps, mountains, forests and vast savannah game plains – which with its beneficent climate, fertile soils and productive fisheries comprised the very heartland of African humanity: the Bantu-Hima kingdoms.

No inclusive name was ever given to this great inland water system, which, together with its remarkably gifted people, was hidden from the outside world until comparatively recent times. For the purpose of my account, I have ventured to call it the 'Secret Nile'. Its discovery is a story of adventure and idealism – and, as we look back with the benefit of hindsight – of hypocrisy and corrosive culture contacts, that were both pointless and profitless from a British viewpoint. This involvement was to leave twentieth-century Britain with a moral liability, redeemed only by the personal identification and dedication of a few privileged individuals, whose lives became closely associated with one of the most beautiful region of the continent and the most engaging of its peoples.

This identification – as Richard Burton observed, John Hanning Speke exemplified, and Henry Morton Stanley confirmed – is a kind of rising 'madness', peculiar to this part of Africa. As for myself from the day when, as a young soldier, I first marvelled at the Ripon Falls in 1943, I have also suffered from this madness and this book may perhaps be regarded as an attempt at its exorcism.

It has been said that this new century will be the century of Africa; it has also been said that it will be the era of the international struggle for water and so, inescapably, of renewed struggle for the Nile. It is right, therefore, that the state of affairs discovered by our Victorian forebears, and the part they played, for better and for worse, in creating new political entities at the sources of the famous and fabulous river, should be set down for a modern audience. If this generation is to attempt to understand what happened, what is happening and what is *yet* likely to happen in central Africa, it is essential that it appreciates the state of affairs that prevailed when the first contacts with an alien western culture took place. For it is this, rather than the ephemeral intervening few decades of colonial *pax europea*, that inescapably will be the basis of what is to happen in the future. In Africa, particularly, it is true to say that circumstances and outside influences come and go, but there is a hardcore that remains for ever the same and in that hardcore lies hope for the countries of the African continent.

Overleaf: The great lateen sail of an Arab dhow. The design of these craft is practically unchanged since the days of the ivory and slave trade and they are still to be seen in the port of Zanzibar today. This one was photographed on the waters of Lake Victoria.

Drawing Aside the Veil

At the end of the first quarter of the nineteenth century, little more was known about the interior of equatorial Africa and the sources of the Nile than had been written by the ancients of Greece and Rome and the medieval Arabic scholars. The only evidence as to the existence and nature of that vast region, was the irregular trickle of ivory and slaves reaching the shores of the continent. The ivory, *objets d'art*, piano keys, chessmen, knife handles and billiard balls destined for the luxury trade; the slaves for the labour and sex markets of the Islamic world. How thrilling it must have been for the sailors aboard the British frigate, HMS *Leven*, when they took up station for their first tour of duty as an anti-slavery patrol in 1824 and received their first glimpse of the coast. The shore would have been dotted with the white lateen sails of the Arab coastal sailing ships. And, as the British sailors got nearer to the coast, their eyes would have rested on endless silver strands, backed by brilliant vegetation, mangrove, ever-swaying palm, baobab and casuarina, among which were dotted white coral rag houses, covered in purple bougainvillea. The scent of spices and blossom would have reached out to seduce the land-starved voyagers. This enticing picture is only one aspect of Africa, but it is as alluring as it is fraught with danger. It is the bait that may seduce the onlooker when he is at his most susceptible and, in that unguarded moment, the famous madness may befall him and hold him for ever captive. I know...

Slavery remained fundamental to the way of life and the economy of many Islamic countries. Britain's crusade against this trade in human misery had a lot to do with a guilt complex about British past involvement in the West African slave trade with the American colonies. While Britain had little influence over the Ottoman Empire in Constantinople, her naval power meant that she had at least some possibility of restricting the shipment of slaves from the East Coast of Africa to Arabia and the Persian gulf. This trade was carried out under the aegis of the Arabian sultans of Zanzibar, who claimed suzerainty over the continent's equatorial coast but, in the interior, power was in the hands of Arab and Swahili slavers who only acknowledged the authority of the sultans when it was opportunistic to do so.

Every year between twenty to forty thousand slaves were captured in the African interior

Opposite: *This map, the work of the Frenchman, De Fer, was published in 1720. It is based on the discoveries of the Jesuits who visited Abyssinia in the seventeenth century.*

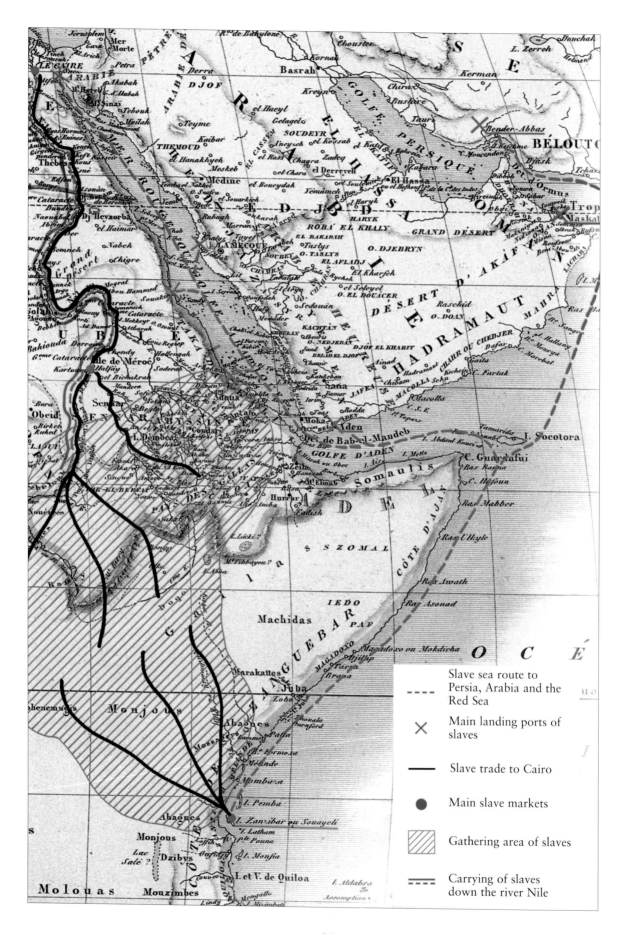

Slave sea route to Persia, Arabia and the Red Sea

Main landing ports of slaves

Slave trade to Cairo

Main slave markets

Gathering area of slaves

Carrying of slaves down the river Nile

and dragged to the small island state of Zanzibar. As the conditions of their transportation and the treatment meted out to them were extremely harsh, mortality was high and the trade was fuelled by a continuous demand, both for work on local plantations and for export. In Zanzibar the sale of slaves in the market place was an almost daily scene. The wealth generated by this human trade allowed the sultans and the merchant settlers to lead a pleasant life indeed. The Arab plantation owners and the slave traders had built themselves grand residences, with shady courtyards and lush gardens, full of fountains. The white traders who had settled on the island – Americans, Germans, Britons and Frenchmen – were frequent guests of the sultans who saw the potential usefulness of these 'infidels'. In the mid-nineteenth century there were around five thousand Arab traders living on Zanzibar, with many owing large clove and coconut plantations. The running of such estates was labour-intensive and relied almost entirely on a free, ever renewable source of labour. Slavery was fundamental to the economies of Islamic states and neither the Arabs nor the Turks considered the trade in 'ebony' immoral. There were risks and expenses involved in the organisation of raids into the wild interior to capture the slaves, or in eluding the European blockade at sea, but the financial rewards from the trade were so great as to make any risk worthwhile.

The British naval patrols were no more than a pinprick in the flank of the Ottoman Empire, but Zanzibar, as a minuscule island state was at the mercy of the British navy. A succession of notable British consuls: Lieutenant-Colonel Atkins Hamerton, Captain Christopher Rigby and John Kirk – the latter would be the Scots protegé and fellow traveller of David Livingstone – maintained the pressure on the Arab sultan rulers of the island, whose lavish lifestyle could only be sustained by unimpeded trade and convinced them that they could little afford to alienate Britain. In 1845 the sultans were finally driven to close the notorious slave market in the town and to declare slavery illegal. Zanzibar, however, remained the entrepot for ivory, a trade controlled by the Indian traders who had settled on the island at the beginning of the nineteenth century, and for incoming trade goods, notably arms, gunpowder; cotton; porcelain and other luxury goods.

Slavery continued to be legal in the Ottoman Empire and there the British and French naval blockade was of little more than cosmetic value. The whole of eastern equatorial Africa, extending far into the Congo basin, was parcelled up under a *de facto* system,

Opposite: This French map shows the two principal slave routes used during the eighteenth and nineteenth century. The slavers ascended the White Nile and its Abyssinian tributaries, slaves captured in those areas were sent to Khartoum, from there to be taken to the markets of Cairo. The island of Zanzibar performed a smilar role, sending slaves to Persia and Arabia.

whereby a stronger tribe took captives and ivory from its weaker neighbours and sold them to Arab slavers in exchange for arms and cloth. The trade in ivory and in slaves dovetailed handily. The slaves themselves were used to carry the ivory to the coast. There, they were loaded on to boats which the blockading ships had little hope of intercepting on the high seas. This moral and humanitarian challenge, coupled with the great religious revival in mid-nineteenth-century Britain that gave rise to a great wave of missionary fervour, became the prime incentive for the exploration of eastern Africa by Europeans. The moral and religious motives also coalesced with the romantic and scientific search for the Nile sources. This rich agenda would prove to be a highly effective motivation to missionaries and explorers alike.

One positive outcome of the repulsive slave trade was that the Arab merchants had for centuries penetrated far and wide into the interior of the continent and had collected some information on the terrain and peoples of these regions. As European travellers and scholars were gripped by the obsession for the quest for the sources of the Nile, it was per force to the accounts of Arab scholars and merchants that they turned to for information.

Below: The lofty panorama of the Zanzibar coast concealed the sordid reality of the almost daily ritual of the slave market, shown on the page opposite.

It is unusual to seek the source of a river other than by following it upstream from its mouth. For two thousand years this had been the favoured approach: upstream from the Mediterranean, a process simplified by the lack of tributaries to the main river. But the travellers could only proceed up to a point, eventually they met an impenetrable barrier of floating reeds and weeds – the Sudd – which vitiated all their efforts. By the middle of the nineteenth century, however, this apparently impenetrable obstacle was breached by the Arabs, who, in turn, became the obstacle to European advance into that region. Arab enterprise from the north, ostensibly under the control of Turkey and Egypt as overlords but, in practice, freebooting under the anarchy of Khartoum, had pushed expeditions beyond the marshes, to exploit the untapped reservoirs of ivory and black slaves to be found in the region of the Nile headwaters. Such slave masters and their trains of armed local Sudanese had no interest in solving geographical mysteries; but they had a strong incentive to prevent the ingress of Europeans, with their incomprehensible objections to the slaving business. This was the new obstacle that confronted western travellers and closed the approach to the Nile sources.

As mentioned before, apart from the Greek merchant Diogenes's account of his journey into the interior from the east coast 2000 years earlier – as recorded by Marinus of Tyre and Claudius Ptolemy – there was no record of a European attempt to penetrate eastern equatorial Africa until the year 1824. At that time, a British naval officer, Captain W F E Owen, commanding HMS *Leven*, was engaged in making a hydrographical survey of the coast for the anti-slave squadron and, as a result of involvement with the ruling Mazrui slaving family, he was incautiously led into declaring a British protectorate over the small in-shore city island of Mombasa, an action that was soon revoked by the British government. But, while the short-lived protectorate was in existence, Owen appointed James Reitz, his Lieutenant, as Resident. This enterprising officer seized the opportunity to make an exploratory journey into the mainland coastal belt. Unfortunately, he died of fever in May 1824. Port Reitz, the great inland basin behind Mombasa Island, commemorates his achievement, and it is fitting that he should be recognised as the first European traveller into east Africa.

Reitz was succeeded by Lieutenant James Emery who, in conversation with local people, heard of a great lake with densely populated shores, lying far inland. Emery brought this to the notice of the Royal Geographical Society through Desborough Cooley, who was an early proponent of the 'Great-Lake Nile-source' hypothesis. Cooley tried vainly to persuade the Society to support Emery on a new expedition, but the latter's estimate of the costs involved proved too onerous.

There is no record of another European attempt into the mainland until 1845, when Lieutenant Maizan, a twenty-five-year old officer aboard the French warship *La Dordogne*, conceived the idea of a solo equatorial crossing of the continent.

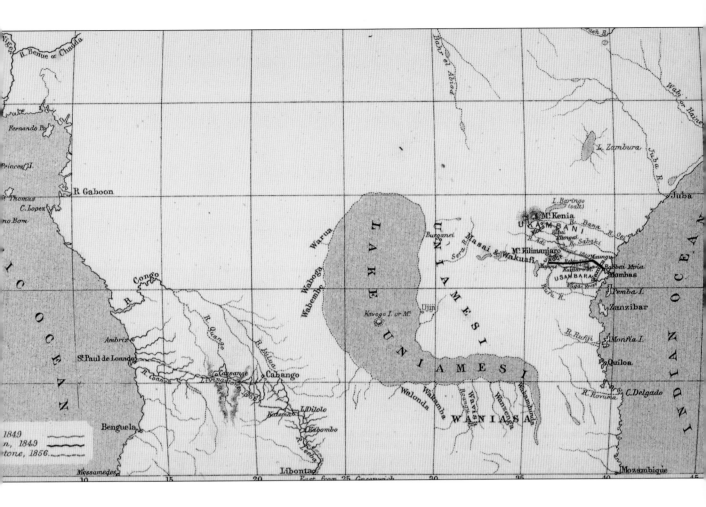

His expedition was officially sanctioned in France and Zanzibar, but Maizan had more enthusiasm than organisational skills and he was murdered after only 129 km (80 miles).

In European minds, this misadventure confirmed the belief that it was sheer folly to engage with this apparently useless and savage land. Yet, even as the tragedy occurred, another event took place which was to have profound consequences. The German Protestant missionary, Johann Ludwig Krapf, who was working under the aegis of the English Church Missionary Society, arrived in Zanzibar in 1844, having been rebuffed in his original purpose of proselytising the Coptic Christians of Abyssinia. In 1845 he set up house on the island of Mombasa, with his wife Rosina, and their baby daughter, both of whom would shortly die of fever. In 1846 he was joined by an English-ordained German, Johann Rebmann, with whom he built the famous mission station at Rabai Mpya (New Rabai), on what was regarded as a healthier site in the Rabai hills, 24 km (15 miles) inland from Mombasa island. They were the first European residents on the mainland.

Above. *The so-called 'Slug Map' which fired the imagination of nineteenth-century geographers and travellers.*

It was these two men who turned Victorian geography upside down with their successive discoveries of snow-capped mountains on the Equator: Mount Kilimanjaro was discovered by Rebmann on 11th May 1848 and Mount Kenya by Krapf, on 3rd December 1849. The presence of snow on the equator was challenged, not only by Cooley, but also by the President of the Royal Geographical Society, Sir Roderick Murchison, supported by the esteemed Dr David Livingstone. They concluded that 'the missionaries…may have been deceived by the glittering aspect of quartz rocks under a tropical sun.' Luckily, another eminent academic, J M McQueen, accepted the snow mountains and, understandably, the erroneous assumption was made that the mountains formed part of the snowy sources of the Nile, so tantalizingly evoked by Herodotus.

Soon after his discovery, Krapf was invalided home and Rebmann was joined by another young missionary, J J Erhardt, who shared his interest in geography. By questioning Arab travellers, Rebmann and Erhardt, pieced together information suggesting that, were a traveller to strike inland from the coast, after a few months, he would eventually come to an inland freshwater sea. This theory appeared to confirm Emery's report, although his name does not seem to have been mentioned in connection with Rebmann and Erhardt's findings. In 1855, the two men drew a speculative map of this lake, reputedly some 1,287 km (800 miles) long, curling and slug-like in shape. This so-called 'slug map' appeared in the *Nouvelles Annales de Voyages*, published in 1856. (See page 25.)

The map was speculative, it added no new facts or concrete knowledge to the strange mixture of part-facts, part-fiction which had been tossed about for centuries past, yet it made a great impression. Reports of the map reached the Royal Geographical Society in London, at about the same time as the thrilling news of Livingstone's crossing of southern central Africa, during the years 1853 to 1856, when he followed the Zambezi river upstream and discovered the Victoria Falls.

An explosion of interest in the geography of central Africa ensued. The Slug Sea, known to the Arabs as the Sea of Ujiji or Unyamwezi, from the names of their settlements on its eastern side, was seen as a prime candidate for the Nile source. The Royal Geographical Society was determined that Britain should have the glory of finding the sources of the Nile. Livingstone was persuaded to return to Africa to seek the southern end of the Slug Sea. In due course he discovered Lake Nyasa (Lake Malawi), but it turned out to be an affluent of the Zambezi river, which ruled it out as a possible source of the Nile. Although Livingstone continued his lonely travels for many years, they were to prove rather unproductive: he never actually set foot in the Nile basin. Historically he was destined to be only a marginal player in the great Nile game. But, as Britain was recovering from the trauma of the Crimean War (1853-56), the stage was set for a new and dynamic initiative in the field of African exploration.

The Discovery of
Lake Tanganyika

1857-1859

Who was to seek out the Slug Sea? There existed no pool of experienced British explorers familiar with the huge tract of land involved, but there was an outstanding figure who had travelled extensively in Arabia and Somaliland: Sir Richard Francis Burton, a captain in the Indian Army and a man of considerable intellectual stature. Burton was one of the great Victorians and, in some ways, one of the most attractive. It is conventional to list those of his many gifts that could be safely mentioned in polite society: he was a linguist, anthropologist, orientalist, writer, translator and poet. He was also a courageous man, a modernist, well ahead of his time. But he had a demonic counter-ego: he was a restless, cynical egocentric, who took pleasure in other peoples' discomfiture. Even more shocking in Victorian eyes: he was an amoralist and atheist; a sexual adventurer and an eroticist, verging on the pornographer; a sadist and racist; a drinker and a rake. His was a personality filled with contradictions, yet he was attractive to women, although his sexual orientation appears to have been ambivalent. His relationship with Isabel Arundell, with whom he contracted a lasting but childless marriage, was one of the great romances of the age, but there is some doubt as to the exact nature of their physical relationship.

On an expedition to Somalia, Burton had been accompanied by three Indian Army brother officers: Captain John Hanning Speke and Lieutenants Stroyan and Herne. Attacked by natives at night, Stroyan was killed and Burton received a spear thrust through his face, leaving a scar which shows clearly in the superb portrait, painted by Sir Frederick Leighton (page 29). Only Herne escaped unharmed, while Speke was left severely wounded.

Captain John Hanning Speke's character was in many ways the antithesis of Burton's. His equal in courage, but surpassing him in fortitude, endurance and persistence, he lacked Burton's interest in the lives of the people and the languages of Africa. He seems to have been sexually negative and, although professedly simple, honest and straightforward, he was as contorted in the depths of his mind as Burton, and capable of being even more devious. Moreover, although the two men regarded each other as friends, each felt himself superior to the other and it would seem impossible to find two less compatible fellow travellers. Speke might not have been Burton's first choice on an hazardous expedition through uncharted territory, and it was probably only their common burning desire to grasp the Nile prize that made their companionship possible – a unity of purpose that in the end was to destroy them both. Such was the ill-starred foundation on which rested what was to be the most important expedition in the history of the search for the Nile sources.

What was known of the vast stretch of Africa, which the two men were committing themselves to cross? Apart from the two snow-capped mountains, glimpsed from afar by the German missionaries, and the hypothetical Slug Sea, the map of eastern Africa was a blank. From the scanty information gleaned from Arab reports, all the explorers knew, was that after weeks of struggle though humid, unhealthy and swampy vegetation, they would ascend a rugged escarpment to reach a plateau, characterised by dessicated thorn-bush offering no protection from the torrid sun and little in the way of fresh water. Only after several months of travel through this hostile environment, could they expect the landscape to change to a monotonous woodland, leafless for most of the year, before they had a hope, finally, of reaching the freshwater sea.

Burton and Speke reached Zanzibar at the end of 1856 and proceeded to organise a caravan. In their ignorance they purchased a large number of donkeys, when they found themselves unable to recruit porters in sufficient numbers. This led to a decision which was to have incalculable consequences: Burton had brought along a galvanised iron boat, the *Louisa*, which had been constructed in England for the purpose of exploring the inland sea. Designed to come apart into sections, each weighing forty pounds – a light load for a porter – the boat was a most practical piece of equipment. It was named after one of Burton's old love, Louisa, a beautiful cousin of his then fiancée, Isabel. In naming the boat after his past love rather than for the sake of his future wife, Burton was being characteristically insensitive. But the fates were on Isabel's side, for in what seems to have been a panic-stricken moment of load shedding, the *Louisa* was left behind and forgotten, an action which was to have dire consequences.

Little did they know but, as they assembled their small caravan on the mainland, just south of the slave port of Bagamoyo, Burton and his companions were improvising and inventing something totally new, at least in terms of European experience: the *safari* (the word itself was borrowed from the Swahili for 'travel'). The first requirement for such an enterprise is a good headman, and here, fortune favoured Burton in the unlikely shape of an excruciatingly ugly ex-slave, Sidi Mubarak Bombay, who subsequently served with Speke and Grant, and later on with Stanley. The important part played by this man in the field of African exploration has now been recognised. Even at the time, Speke

Opposite: *Sir Richard Francis Burton, from the painting by Lord Leighton, 1876. The scar on Burton's cheek was the legacy of a spear thrust, received during the ill-fated expedition to Somaliland in 1854.*

acknowledged Bombay's outstanding qualities, even if his praise sounds rather embarrassing to modern ears: 'I never saw any black man so thoroughly honest and conscientious...a regular Man Friday.' The expedition's plan was to follow the established slave route, across the centre of the Tanganyika territory, to the Arab settlement of Kazeh (modern Tabora) and on to Ujiji on the inland sea, a little south of modern Kigoma.

They set off on 27th June 1857. Burton and Speke were experienced travellers, but they were not prepared for the tensions within their column, caused by the bickering and animosity between their porters and the escort of Baluchi soldiers, on whose presence the Sultan had insisted. The two explorers were also ill-prepared for the travelling conditions. In nineteenth-century India and in Somaliland, Europeans and their native entourage travelled in the saddle, whether on horse or camel. But now they found themselves in a world where the prevalence of the tsetse fly – one of the many types of blood-sucking flies that transmit a variety of diseases, especially sleeping sickness – dictated that there was only one reliable means of progress: one's own legs, while the only reliable beast of burden was the porters' strong backs. Donkeys were an ineffectual substitute, and none of them survived beyond the outward journey.

Expeditions of this type call for special skills in human management, something in which both Burton and Speke proved surprisingly deficient, in spite of their army background. They were also highly susceptible to the omnipresent malarial fever. Their journey is a sorry tale of recurring sickness, desertions, losses and of impositions by petty chiefs – all these pressures to be borne by two men who were increasingly irritated by each other's company, yet who were absolutely dependent on each other, as they were almost constantly ill. This was long before it was discovered that malaria is transmitted by mosquito bites and no preventive measures could be taken. Interestingly, on an earlier journey, Burton had speculated that malaria might be 'caused' by mosquitoes – a perceptive suggestion that anticipated by some 50 years James Ross's famous work in India. Sadly Burton did not put his theory to effective use. The empirical use of natural quinine was known, but not its strategic use to *pre-empt* fever. They took far too small a supply with them and used it ineffectively.

The landscape through which they travelled for 225 days, across half the width of the continent, is certainly harsh. I know it well, having traversed it several times. The coastal belt is heavily vegetated, hot, humid and enervating, but it eventually gives way to a range of low hills. These form the eastern escarpment of the continental plateau and, as the traveller ascends them, he witnesses a radical change in the aspect of

Opposite: The map shows Burton and Speke's route to Lake Tanganyika and Speke's solitary journey which gave him his first glimpse of Lake Victoria.

Speke's 1st view

White Nile

Albert Nile

Lake Turkana

Victoria Nile

Mt Elgon

Semliki R.

Rwenzori Mts

Mt Kenya

Equator

R. Tana

Virunga Volcanoes

Nairobi

Kagera R.

L. Victoria

Mwanza

Mt Kilimanjaro

Krapf

Rusizi

Speke

Mt Kilimanjaro

Rebmann

Rabai

Uvira

Mombasa

UNYAMWEZI

Burton and Speke

Kazeh

Ujiji

0   100

miles

UGOGO

Bagamoyo

Zanzibar

Mpwapwa

L. Tanganyika

GHY

the landscape. For most of the year, this region, known as Gogoland after its inhabitants – the Wagogo people – is desperately lacking in shade and water. But, for all its harshness, it possesses a stark beauty, with its strange candelabra and baobab trees, its weirdly sculptured rock kopjes – the bones of Africa's ancient granites revealed by erosion – and its distant blue hills. As one travels westwards, an open canopy of deciduous woodland, known as *miombo* develops, extending throughout the western half of the country. This is a depressing region for most of the year, especially at the very worst of the leafless drought, when the *miombo* appears as if life on this part of the earth was almost extinct. Yet, miraculously, as the rains approach, the desolate terrain changes overnight and becomes arrayed in scarlet – not by flowers – but by tiny leaf buds. Within a week or two, as the rains arrive, the most extraordinary colour shift takes place: bronze to pale gold, followed at last by fresh green – a colour cascade no less impressive for being in reverse, than the North American fall.

In the heart of this western *miombo* country, after 134 days of struggle, Burton and Speke reached the Arab settlement of Kazeh, which is now the Provincial capital, Tabora. Among their many incompatibilities, was Burton's affinity for Islamic culture of which Speke was both ignorant and contemptuous. Burton's knowledge of Arabic enabled him to question the widely travelled and thoughtful Arabs and he soon realised that the Slug Sea was in fact three separate bodies of water: the Nyasa to the south, the Ujiji or Unyamwezi to the west and the Nyanza, or Sea of Ukerewe, to the north. The words – Nyasa, Nyanza and other variants – refer to any large body of water. On hearing this report of the northern sea, Speke tried to persuade Burton to make it their first objective, but Burton insisted on sticking to their original plan. This was the second in a series of critical errors in what was to become a saga of misjudgement.

Refreshed by the Arabs' hospitality, but still in deteriorating health, their donkeys almost finished and their porters ever more reluctant, Burton and Speke still had many weeks of travel before them. On 13th February 1858, 225 days after leaving the coast, their tattered column descended from a range of low hills. Burton, his legs paralysed, was being carried in a hammock; Speke, almost blind with an eye infection, was riding their last donkey that collapsed and died under him on that very day. Miraculously, as everything seemed doomed, suddenly, below them, they saw a streak of light – it was the Sea of Ujiji – Lake Tanganyika.

They had found the lake, but now they had to determine what part, if any, it played in the geography of the Nile. It was imperative for them to sail to the north, where they hoped to find the outlet of the lake. Their massive blunder in leaving their boat, the *Louisa*, behind, now came home to roost. The only possibility open to them was to attempt the lake journey by means of native dug-out canoes, although these were suitable for little else than in-shore fishing. Nonetheless, they obtained two, sailed north, crossing to the western shore and reaching a market place called Uvira, near the lake head. At that point their crewmen refused to go any further due to reports of cannibals. Burton and Speke had however reached far enough to see that the head of the lake was walled in by a grand cirque of forested mountains, some 2,134 m (7,000 ft) in height. Their hopes were dashed by the sight and by the unequivocal assurance of the locals that there was no river flowing out to the north. In fact, the only river to be found in the region, the substantial Rusizi, flowed *into* the lake, not out of it. Speke, the expedition's surveyor, had already calculated the altitude of the lake surface to be only 548 m (1,800 ft) above sea level, far too low to make it a possible contender for the Nile. Most of Speke's surveying instruments had been lost during the journey. He had to improvise and did not realise that his rudimentary apparatus – he was reduced to using a common bath thermometer to determine the boiling point of water which, when using a proper hypsometer, determines the altitude – had given him seriously inaccurate computations. In fact, the true altitude of Lake Tanganyika is about 762 m (2,500 ft): not altogether inconceivable for a source of the Nile. Again, with hindsight, we can see that Burton's failure to convince the porters to press on for the remaining distance – less than 16 km (10 miles), as it turned out – and to confirm by actual inspection the status of the river Rusizi, was yet another crucial mistake. In his defence it must be said that his judgement may have been impaired by bad health. He was plagued by severe mouth ulcers that prevented him from speaking or from taking solid food. Speke too was ill. He was suffering agonies from an accidentally self-inflicted trauma to his eardrum, that was to leave him permanently deaf.

Below: In this naive watercolour, Speke recorded the valleys and mountains encountered by him and Burton on their journey towards Lake Tanganyika.

In low spirits, they set about the hazardous return journey to Ujiji, when a dramatic lake storm nearly overwhelmed them. They survived, however, and in fact the sea journey and the bracing air improved their health. After making a safe landfall, they were soon able to start back for Kazeh. Although they were not entirely unappreciative of the beauty and grandeur of their discovery, their accounts are so weighted by the memory of their various misfortunes, that only a muted picture emerges. In truth, Lake Tanganyika is one of the jewels of Africa. In my opinion, it exceeds all the other great lakes in loveliness and nobility. It measures 644 km (400 miles) in length and is 33 to 65 km (20 to 40 miles) wide (say up to twice the width of the Straits of Dover). It is immensely deep. At over 1,229 m (4000 ft), it is second in the world only to Lake Baikal. Set amongst thrilling mountains, it is the ultimate in rift-valley lakes, even surpassing its splendid congener, Lake Malawi. Often a deep cornflower blue, Lake Tanganyika will change subtly to aquamarine or palest green and, suddenly, to an ominous grey, indicative of an impeding storm. Then the rapid darkening of the waters, the racing white horses and the notorious waterspouts, can be frightening and life-threatening.

By the time the two men reached Kazeh and the Arabs' warm welcome, Burton, who was still plagued by leg weakness, was unfit for anything but rest, and the thing he was best at: talking to their hosts and painstakingly recording their accounts of the ethnography and languages of the regions they had visited. This was an occupation from which Speke was excluded by his inability to speak Arabic. But he was by now so improved in health, that when the Arabs repeated their assertion that there was another great sea, the Nyanza or Sea of Ukerewe, only about sixteen days-march to the north, Speke proposed that they should *both* make this extra expedition. Burton, for some reason, rejected the idea, and, when Speke then proposed that *he* should make a solo trip, Burton raised no objection. This was to be the greatest of all of his repeated errors of judgement.

Below: Hill view

The Discovery of
Lake Victoria

1858–1859

On 9th July 1858 John Hanning Speke, Mubarak Bombay and a small caravan set out from Kazeh. A comparatively easy journey, lasting only a few weeks, brought them to Lake Victoria, the largest lake in the old world – only Lake Superior in America has a greater superficies. This journey and the discovery of the lake would eventually make Speke's name imperishable as the discoverer of the source of the Nile, but I anticipate, as this happened only after years of tears and bitterness and Speke's premature death.

As the party set off from Kazeh on the first few marches to the north, they were still among the unpopulated tsetse-fly-infested *miombo* woodland. Passing the village of Kahama (a modern district centre), they left the land of the great Wanyamwezi tribe behind and, on 26th July, they commenced an imperceptible descent. Speke could hardly have realised it, but that day's march carried him across the watershed: he had entered the Nile catchment at its southerly limit. Eventually, the woodland gave way to open grasslands, leading on to one of the most extensive fertile regions of Africa – what is called the Sukumaland cultivation steppe – the homeland of the numerous Wasukuma people. This is country that I have lived in and got to know well. It is plainsman's country, ocean-like rolling waves of sunlit land, topped by picturesque granite tors, seemingly the work of a titanic Henry Moore. The skyscapes are breathtaking, with massive cumulus and tropical anvil clouds, producing a delightful dappling of the landscape. The density of human population and of the vast herds of cattle was of a quite different order than anything they had encountered in the regions to the east, with which they were already familiar. Speke was the first to realise that this lake region comprised the heartland of African humanity. One can sense the elevation of his spirits as, day by day, on the back of a mule borrowed from the Arabs, his journey towards his great discovery becomes a celebration.

On 30th July 1858, he writes: '…facing to the left, I could discern a sheet of water about [7 km] four miles from me, which ultimately proved to be a creek and the most southerly point of the Nyanza… This I maintain was *the* discovery of the source of the Nile.' He was looking at the easternmost reach, since known as Stuhlmann Sound, of the magnificent 80-km(fifty-miles) long inlet or ria, which later came to be called Smith Sound.

As he marched north, along the eastern side of Smith Sound, he discovered that it

increased in width and was dotted with islands that reminded him of the Greek archipelago. This reach is known now as Mwanza Gulf and it is indeed one of the most attractive spots of the lake region. On 2nd August he reached the village of Isamiro from where the view to the north was obscured by a range of low bush-covered hills.

Next day, on 3rd August 1858, he writes: 'The caravan, after quitting Isamiro, began winding up a long but gradually inclined hill...until it reached its summit, when the vast expanse of the pale blue waters of the Nyanza burst suddenly upon my gaze.' Anyone who has been privileged to stand upon that spot – as my family and I often did, for we once lived in a house on Isamiro hill, overlooking the lake – can understand the surge of joy in his heart. Speke's conviction that he had won the prize, ie discovered the source of the Nile, came upon him with the intensity of a religious revelation. The discovery meant everything to him and Providence had conspired that it should be his alone. 'I no longer felt any doubt that the lake at my feet gave birth to that interesting river, the source of which has been the subject of so much speculation and the object of so many explorers.' Yet, even at this transcendent moment, the seeds of the forthcoming controversy were being sewn.

Speke's difficulty was that, at the time, he had no scientific proof to back his conviction and it is little surprising that many of his contemporaries regarded his emotional utterances and his claims as sheer madness. Because of this, Speke's discovery became tarnished by bitter controversy, although his conviction that he had stumbled upon the true source of the Nile would turn out to be true. The intervening years of conflict and controversy were not so much about what was the truth, but what, on the basis of the available evidence, a rational man had a right to believe was true.

Speke's first glimpse of the lake must have been from the dip in the range, about 1,500 km (1 mile) north of the present lake port of Mwanza. A laden caravan would of course have crossed the hills by the lowest col, not the tops. It would have been a grand view, although circumscribed. Only to the north-west is there a true sea horizon, an arc of about 60 degrees which, given the modest altitude of Speke's viewpoint, can only have commanded some 65 km (40 miles) of water. From an outsider's point of view, he had no factual justification for claiming the discovery of a lake any more extensive than this, and there was certainly no evidence of a river that could conceivably be the Nile.

The logical step at this stage would have been to set sail upon the waters to find out just how far they extended and whether there was an outlet that could possibly be the Nile.

Opposite: The typical thatched roof of a hut in Sukumaland, an ostrich egg and the shells of large snails have been placed at the apex as fertility symbols.
Overleaf: Fishing boats near Mwanza

But, as with Lake Tanganyika earlier on, the absence of the *Louisa* prevented them from carrying out this vital reconnaissance work, while the local canoes were either unsuitable, or Speke and his men failed to find ways of using them. (Some years later, Stanley was to show that canoes from the nearby island of Ukerewe were capable of making such a journey.) But the mainland Wasukuma people were timid inshore fishermen, and it must be remembered that the body of water in question, was of a greater extent than the Irish sea, with all its potential for danger. The first thing Speke did during his three-day stay on the lakeshore was to use his improvised apparatus to attempt once again to determine the altitude of the lake. It gave an altitude of about 1,220 m (4,000 feet) – a reading not very far wrong from the correct one and encouraging from his point of view, since it was compatible with the Nile theory. Next, he consulted the local people – as well as he could – bearing in mind his almost total ignorance of the language. None of the fishermen were long-distance seafarers, but the consensus was that 'the sea extended for many months, probably to the edge of the world.' An impressive affirmation, but not one likely to carry much weight with Britain's sceptical armchair geographers. Considering the magnitude and potential importance of his discovery, one cannot fail to be astonished by how little effort Speke made to prove the accuracy of his theory and by his over-hasty wish to get back to Burton at Kazeh.

The sardonic Burton's reaction to Speke's enthusiastic and bombastic report was a taste of things to come. Burton, to say the least, was far from impressed. When Speke dropped his bombshell, upon his return to Kazeh, Burton's sarcasm was scathing. 'We had scarcely breakfasted,' he wrote, 'before he announced to me the startling fact that he had discovered the source of the White Nile. It was an inspiration perhaps…The fortunate discoverer's conviction was strong; his reasons were weak – were of the category alluded to by the damsel Lucetta, when justifying her penchant in favour of the "lovely gentleman" Sir Proteus:

"I have no other reason but a woman's reason.
I think him so because I think him so."'

Speke's proposal that they should return together to inspect the lake, regardless of their poor state of health and the various logistical problems involved, was dismissed out of hand by Burton, who thus threw away his last card. The subject was dropped and, in silent acrimony, they set about the terrible four-month journey back to the coast. Their mutual animosity was not helped by the fact that, desperately ill in turn, they had no alternative but to nurse each other with tender intimacy!

From Zanzibar they took passage to Aden, but when immediate berths for Britain were offered them aboard a visiting Royal Navy vessel, HMS *Furious*, Burton, who had met an old friend, opted to stay behind for a few days. It is obvious that he was making it ostentatiously plain that neither he nor Speke had news of sufficient import to make them hurry home. This was yet another mistake on Burton's part, for Speke accepted the offer of the berth. Yet in spite of their deep-seated animosity, the two men were still on formally courteous terms and, according to Burton, Speke's last words to him (they were indeed his very last words to him) were: 'Goodbye old fellow; you may be quite sure that I will not go up to the Society until you come to the fore, and we appear together. Make your mind quite easy about that.' In a subsequent letter from Cairo, Speke renewed that promise.

Up to the moment when Speke boarded HMS *Furious*, it is difficult not to feel sympathy for him. Burton emerges as a tiresomely arrogant know-all of a companion, while Speke's attitude could be described as polite and courageous, if sometimes smug and clumsy. Alas, through a chance meeting on the deck of the ship, all that was to change. Also on board was Laurence Oliphant, an odious member of the chattering classes. He was secretary to Lord Elgin, and they were on their way back from China. Oliphant was a travel journalist and a correspondent for *The Times*. As is the fashion nowadays, modern biographers have implied that Oliphant was bisexual and suggested an aggregation with Speke who, they claim, was mother-obsessed and whose negative sexuality was ostensibly substituted by a passion for the aggressive shooting of wild animals. Whatever the actual chemistry was between the two men, at the end of the voyage, Speke, for the first time, behaved completely out of character, either as an officer or as a gentleman. Although he knew that Burton would reach London a few days after him and, in spite of his promise, he went straight to Sir Roderick Murchison, the President of the Royal Geographical Society, and registered his claim to priority with the discovery of the Nile source. Sir Roderick asked him to address the Society and at once set in motion plans to send him back with an independent command, to complete the exploration of the lake and determine the status of its outlet in respect of the Nile. When Burton reached England ten days later, he found that the wind had been taken out of his sails and that little interest was elicited by his account of the discovery of Lake Tanganyika. His achievements were put firmly in the shade by Speke's far greater 'success'. It must have been particularly galling for Burton, as he himself had written to the Society from Aden. His letter arrived in London three days before Speke's return (presumably by overland mail) and in it Burton treated Speke's claim even-handedly.

'Captain Speke will lay before you his maps and observations and two papers [concerning] his exploration of the Nyanza, Ukerewe or Northern Lake...To this,' Burton wrote, 'I would respectfully direct the serious attention of the Committee as there are grave reasons for believing it to be the source of the principal feeder of the White Nile.' Especially in view of his initial scepticism, he could scarcely have written more fairly. But the lukewarm public reaction to his own announcement, the atmosphere of contention that was already gathering and his anger at Speke's broken promise, soon caused Burton to abandon his rational attitude.

Burton was not without his own supporters and, within a few days, the establishment in Britain was divided into two camps who treated each other's rival claim with increasing vituperation. Burton ill advisedly fell back on the Tanganyika theory: native reports suggested the existence of a chain of lakes running northwards, far to the west of Speke's Nyanza (we now know these to be the rift-valley lakes of Kivu, Edward and Albert). Might not these bodies of water comprise the main course of the Nile? By now Burton regretted bitterly his failure to complete the exploration of the head of Lake Tanganyika, but he was comforted when a recalibration of Speke's improvised hypsometer gave the altitude of Tanganyika as over 762 m (2,500 feet). This figure reinforced Burton's conviction, as it marked the lake as a possible contender for a Nile reservoir.

Subsequently, irrespective of Sir Roderick Murchison's personal preference for Speke, Burton was also asked to submit a plan, and both men were given a fair hearing before the Council of the Society. But whatever the arguments raging in London's clubland, the die had been cast in Speke's favour and the embittered Burton was left on the sidelines of the Nile drama for the rest of his life.

Below: The town of Gondokoro in the Sudan had been an old slave trading centre. It became the starting point of most nineteenth-century explorers, as they made their way into the interior.

The Heart of Darkness

1860-1862

As a companion for his new journey, Speke chose an officer friend of his own age, Captain James Grant of the Indian Army, a thoroughly reliable Scot and totally lacking Burton's hubris. If Speke was looking for someone guaranteed not to upstage him, he could not have done better. Their plan was once more to go to Kazeh, but from there to make a traverse by a western land-route, as reported by the Arabs, and to seek the northern outlet of Lake Victoria. Having found it, they would then follow the river downstream to the north, until they reached the most southerly outpost of the Equatorial Province of the Egyptian-ruled Sudan, a place called Gondokoro, situated on the White Nile. They were contemplating a long walk, a very long walk indeed, of some 3,200 km (2,000 miles).

The plan was that by the time they reached Gondokoro, after travelling for some estimated 18 months, the two men would then be in need of fresh supplies and of water transport. Speke and Grant had come to know John Petherick, who was the then authority on the Sudan Nile and its western reaches, the Bahr-el-Ghazal. For the past 15 years, Petherick had travelled through the region, trading ivory and acting as peripatetic Consul on behalf of the small British community in Khartoum. He had come to Britain in July 1859, where he established a warm relationship, both with Sir Roderick Murchison and the then recently returned Speke. As a result he twice visited Speke's home, Jordans in Somerset, the second time in the company of James Grant.

During these visits, the two men had the opportunity to discuss their plans in detail with Petherick, who warned them that although he had never actually visited the place, he knew that Arab boats were to be found at Gondokoro, but only in the months of December and January. As a result Speke proposed that Petherick himself should organize for boats and supplies to be at Gondokoro, when they arrived. In due course, Speke wrote to Petherick on 22nd December 1859, and his words were to prove prophetic: 'What a jolly good thing it would be to accomplish. You could do your ivory business at the same time that you work out the geography!!'

The Royal Geographical Society came up with only minimal financial sponsorship – £1,000 – for Petherick, which he estimated 'would barely suffice to place two well provisioned boats under the superintendence of one of my own men…[and] to await the arrival of the expedition…from November 1861 until June 1862.' The rendezvous was to take place on the west bank of the river. The agreement included the proviso that 'in the event of Captain Speke not having arrived by that time at Gondokoro,

Consul Petherick shall not be bound to remain beyond June 1862.' [My italics]

By August 1860 Speke and Grant had arrived in Zanzibar and on 2nd October they
started inland from Bagamoyo, up the familiar road to Kazeh, which they reached after
116 days. The regions through which they now had to pass: Usui and Uzinza (Kahama
and Biharamulo districts), were under the authority of chiefs who proved so rapacious
that progress became almost impossible and, on several occasions, the African members
of the expedition begged the two men to give up. It is a matter for commendation,
that during the whole of this period of extreme aggravation, not a shot was fired, nor
a single person harmed. To the problems caused by the locals and the need for relays,
were added the bouts of recurring ill-health that plagued the two explorers and conspired
to separate them for long periods. Only the exceptional synergy existing between Speke
and Grant made it possible for them to endure the frustrations and hardships of what
was to be the worst part of the whole journey.

Their progress were still painfully slow. Grant was repeatedly prostrated by fever, but
at least this was something they were familiar with. Poor Speke became much more
seriously ill with a cough that seemed to have developed into a dry pleurisy. Unable
to rest, he was driven to distraction and made various desperate attempts at self-
medication. These included asking his servant, Baraka, to drive a packing needle used
as a seton, into his side. Fortunately, the needle was too blunt 'whereupon I made Baraka
fire me, for the coughing was so incessant, I could get no sleep.' It seems difficult
to believe that Speke managed to survive the disease, as well as the 'cures'.

In June 1861 they entered the unknown country (the reported Karagwe) to the southwest
of Lake Victoria. Their route from Kazeh to Karagwe took them more or less in
a northwesterly direction. In the dry season, this immense stretch of country is harsh
and unprepossessing. The monotonous woodland trees shed their leaves, the grass is burnt
off, and the only shade is provided by occasional fig and mango trees. Valleys alternate
with ridges crested with huge rounded granite outcrops. This corrugated country
alternates rolling swells of sandstone with mixed grass and woodland, as the westerly
Congo watershed gives way to the northerly drainage into the Nile basin. Speke indicates
on his map, that on this leg of their journey, they were never closer to the (then
uncharted) western shores of the Nyanza than 95 to 110 km (60 to 70 miles) – indeed,
he never mentions the presence of the lake. We now know that he and his companions
passed within 33 km (20 miles) of the waters of what has come to be called the Emin
Pasha Gulf.

Opposite: *The picture on the right shows John Hanning Speke. James Augustus Grant is
sitting on the left. These portraits capture something of the two men's character. Grant
was often overawed by Speke and was the perfect travel companion for him.*

At last, they escaped the clutches of the grasping Chief Suwarora of Uzinza and, soon, the whole character of their journey changed. The King of Karagwe, Rumanika, had sent them messages expressing pleasurable anticipation and, on 17th November, they met a party of his officers, who had been sent to welcome them. Things were looking up. From then on their path was made easy, all exactions ceased and food and carriers were provided. This coincided with a delightful change in the landscape. The beautiful Lohugati valley, with its well watered sides, luxuriant vegetation and inviting streams, was followed by the modestly sized lake of Burigi (an ancient branch of the Nyanza) and its game plains, while the increasing altitude, as they ascended the grassy hills of Karagwe, induced optimism: 'Oh, how we enjoyed it!' Speke wrote. There is indeed something special about the skyscape of Karagwe district and most people who have been fortunate enough to visit what is now a remote backwater of Africa, will agree with that statement.

Speke and Grant were greeted by King Rumanika at his capital village of Weranhanje (modern Bweranange) on 25th November 1861. The King was an elegant six-footer. He had been brought to the throne eight years earlier through the usual process

of fratricidal savagery that characterised the Bahima tradition of acceding to the throne (see the details of how Mutesa had come to succeed his father in Buganda on page 52). In other ways Rumanika was gentle, wise, intelligent and a perfect host. Speke's eleven-week stay proved to be a valuable period of recoupment. This long pause was required by Bugandan protocol. The next stage of their journey would take Speke and Grant through districts under the control of Mutesa, King of Buganda, and entering his country without his express invitation and personal escort would have been unthinkable .

The travellers' poor state of health proved to be a further obstacle to their departure. Buganda had a rule that sick strangers should not be admitted into their territory. This probably derived from the country's grim experience of smallpox epidemics. How wise was this edict and how dreadfully would the country suffer in due course from its abandonment! But as far as Speke and Grant were concerned, the ban led to a disastrous delay, for in December Grant developed an infection of his right leg, above the knee – evidently a cellulitis – that incapacitated him completely for five months. Finally, on 8th January 1862 Mutesa relented and sent a smartly clothed delegation, under orders to escort the expedition to his capital in the north. The emissaries would brook no delay and Speke realised that it was a case of now or never, even though, it meant leaving Grant behind.

Thus it was that Speke set out for the north alone. Descending from the hills of Karagwe, he came to a substantial river, flowing to the east towards Lake Victoria. At first he named it the Kitangule Kagera, later referring to it as the Alexander Nile. Today, it is simply called the Kagera and it is indeed the main headwater of the Victoria Nile system, in Speke's words: 'draining the high seated springs in the Mountains of the Moon...of 8000 feet [2,938 m] or more.' (Speke's presumed location of the Mountains of the Moon was far removed from that of the Rwenzori range, discovered later by Sir Henry Morton Stanley and to which, nowadays, the romantic term is usually restricted.)

He was entering the southern part of Uddu or Buddu, as it was then known, in the kingdom of Buganda – the country now known as Uganda. The character of the landscape changes as you travel northwards: although lush compared with much of eastern Africa, this landscape presents a somewhat wearisome succession of plains, marshy in the rains, and studded with large termite mounds, each with its euphorbia candelabra tree. For Speke the repetitious crossing of the swamps, often wading chest-deep, was exhausting, and only twice in this part of his journey was he encouraged by a glimpse of the unknown mass of water on his right-hand side. The first time was from

Opposite: This map shows the spot where Speke came upon the northern shore of Lake Victoria on his second journey.

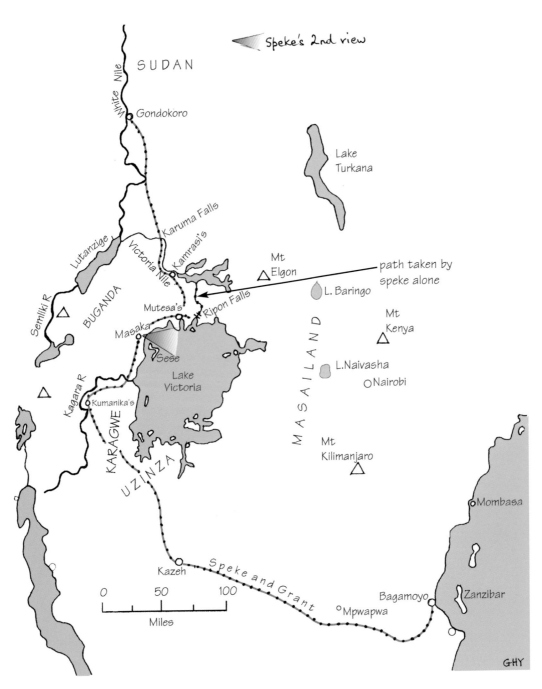

the top of a small hill, south of Masaka. The second time was on 7th of February,
when north of Masaka and extolling the beauty of his surroundings, he describes:
'the long range view it afforded of Uganda proper, the lake and the large group of islands
called Sese.' It is strange how unconcerned he seems to have been, on this crucial section

*Overleaf: The Kagera River. Grant and Speke crossed it on their separate journeys
to Karagwe, but since it flowed into Lake Victoria rather than out of it, they dismissed
it at first as a possible Nile source.*

of his travels, with checking out the shore of the lake and in testing its continuity – a lack of scientific thoroughness that would cause him much trouble later. In fairness, though, it should be remembered that he was restricted by the strict orders which had been given to his royal escort. He did, however, find time to note the well tended gardens of the Baganda, remarking on the lush plantain groves, and the neat conical reed-and-thatch homesteads that were the hallmark of the country.

On 15th February, the escort received instructions to halt their advance and Speke was kept waiting, in his words: 'by Mutesa's arrogance.' One can't help paraphrasing this so-called 'arrogance' as the King's wise caution! But meanwhile, Speke had no alternative but to wait, camped on a hill from which he could see the lake. Eventually, he describes how on the 19th they finally 'came in sight of the King's kibuga', or capital village. Speke noted the precise location in terms of latitude and longitude, not realising that the *kibuga* was not a 'fixed' village. It was wherever the King's handsome but ephemeral reed palace, the *Lubiri*, happened to be erected, and the location of the 'village' therefore changes confusingly as our story develops. Speke goes on describing: 'It was a magnificent sight: a whole hill was covered with gigantic huts, such as I had never seen in Africa before.' February the 19th marks the end of this part of their journey. They had covered the 305 km (190 miles) from Rumanika's territory in less than six weeks.

In the afternoon Speke was conducted through an elaborate complex of reed-fenced courts and anterooms, each sentried gate jingling with bells as it was opened. 'The palace quite surprised me by its extraordinary dimensions and neatness.' It was surrounded by numerous gigantic grass huts, 'thatched as neatly as so many heads dressed by a London barber.' There was a maze of courtyards with yellow reed partitions, the domain of Mutesa's three or four hundred concubines, and there was a cacophony of welcoming musicians and clowns. At last the visitor was admitted to the central *levée* chamber. Mutesa, the *Kabaka*, was seated on a dais in the centre of the space and, since the floor was packed with *wakungu* (senior courtiers), Speke had to squeeze himself at some distance from the king.

Mutesa was a 'good looking well figured tall young man of 25 years, scrupulously clothed in a new mbugu' (bark cloth toga). His hair was cut short except for a high stern-to-stern coxcomb, and he was elegantly arrayed and wore ornaments.' Speke recalled how he 'longed to open conversation but knew not the language…so the King and myself sat staring at one another for a full hour. At last the King sent a spokesman to ask if I had seen him; and on receiving my reply, "Yes, for full one hour" – Mutesa rose and with

Opposite: Life at Mutesa's court was a mixture of sophistication and gross cruelty. In his book, Grant recorded the frequent occurence of prisoners, or of members of the king's entourage who had offended him in some way, being dragged away to be executed.

a comically stilted gait left the chamber.' This 'stilted gait' noted by Speke was restricted to the *Kabaka* and was designed to imitate the noble walk of the lion. (Here it is necessary to explain the prefixes used in the Luganda language: *bu-* refers to the country, *ba-* to the people and *lu-* to the language. Thus *Buganda* is the kingdom, now incorporated into modern Uganda, the *Baganda* are its people and *Luganda* their language.)

Speke set out patiently to win the confidence of the young *Kabaka*. In this, he was helped by the presents he had brought for him. These, ominous portents of the European-African culture clash to come, included a Whitworth rifle, a revolver and three carbines.
A few days later Mutesa asked Speke to demonstrate how the weapons worked. The king then promptly despatched four cows himself, using the revolver. The applause at this feat had scarcely subsided, when Mutesa loaded one of the carbines and, setting it at full cock, gave it to one of his pages with instructions to go outside and shoot someone. To Speke's dismay the order was obeyed straightway, and 'the little urchin returned to announce his success with a look of glee...I never heard, and there appeared to be no curiosity to know, what individual human being the urchin had deprived of life.'

In the Kingdom of Buganda, Speke found himself in a deadly Alice-in-Wonderland world of extraordinary ambivalence. On one hand, there was evidence of social organisation such as he had seen nowhere else in his African travels, not even in Karagwe. Mutesa had a prime minister (the *Katikkiro*), and a cabinet of senior advisers (the *Lukiiko*), with whom he sat daily in council. Each of these had his own sphere of responsibility, either geographical or administrative. Under them was a bureaucracy of more junior

chiefs who managed the affairs of the country. Good order prevailed, houses and courtyards were immaculate, gardens and plantations productive and hunger unknown. Transport on land and on water was also well organised. Hygiene was not ignored, which greatly impressed Speke who wrote: 'the sanitary orders of Uganda required every man to build for himself a house of parliament, such being the neat and cleanly nature of the Waganda – a pattern to all other negro tribes.'

The other side of the coin was that the king had absolute power of life and death over his subjects. Speke was shocked that this power should be expressed with such autocratic brutality. Always in attendance at court were the King's executioners. At a glance from their master, and for the most trifling breaches of protocol, men, women, children were seized and executed. Speke described how: 'Nearly every day…I have seen one, two or three of the wretched palace women led away to execution tied by the hand and dragged along by the body guard, crying out as she went to a premature death.'

The system Speke witnessed must have been in force for several centuries, at least since the inception of the Bahima dynasties. The Baganda had no system of writing. For their history, they and we are dependent on an oral tradition consisting of a tally of the names of some thirty *Kabakas*: this probably sets the first of these rulers in the fifteenth century. On the death of a *Kabaka*, the *Lukiiko* chose one of the sons, who then had to secure his position by slaughtering all his competitor siblings. The only exception was the first born, who, by tradition, could never become *Kabaka*. This explains why Mutesa's eldest brother, Kiwewa, was still alive, a man who, in due course, was to play an active part in the country's affairs. The new *Kabaka* could only sustain his rule by assuming power of life and death over his subjects and the ruthless autocracy at the centre of power may have been a factor contributing to the advanced state this society had achieved in so many areas. Mutesa's kingdom possessed a sophistication far surpassing that of simpler and less autocratic cultures, based on the consensus of village elders, a system prevailing throughout most of Bantu Africa. Sadly these benevolently 'democratic' principles seemed to engender no tangible evidence of societal advance.

The rulers of Buganda, on the other hand, must have also relied on a groundrock of natural ethics which motivated a man such as Mutesa to run a well ordered and prosperous society, as sheer brutal force and complete autocratic power rarely suffice to create and maintain the calm atmosphere described by Speke, at least not in the long run. It is always difficult to understand the mores of societies so different from one's own, and only too easy to romanticize or condemn. In her book, *Moon Tiger*, the writer Penelope Lively, describes how 'the Aztecs, who sacrificed captives to their Gods by carving their living hearts from their bodies, were deeply shocked by the Spanish custom of burning transgressors at the stake.' She concludes sardonically that 'cruelty, evidently, lies in the eyes of the beholder.'

The Discovery of
the Victoria Nile

1862

The first Arab visitors to Buganda had preceded Speke by about 20 years. Noting that
there was some evidence of Islamic influences at Mutesa's court, Speke was anxious
to introduce the subject of Christianity and gave the *Kabaka* a prayer book. It is, however,
debatable as to what degree of real communication can have existed between the two men.
Mutesa at the time did not speak Swahili and Speke was no African linguist. All attempts
at communication must have been through layers of not-too-accurate translation: Speke
to Bombay in Urdu; Bombay to the Arabs and to other coastal travellers in Swahili,
thence to Mutesa's spokesman in Luganda and, finally from this individual to Mutesa
himself, as no other would have dared address the King directly. It is only years later,
when he was a sick, and one may think wiser man, that Mutesa did allow the Arabs
to teach him some Arabic and Swahili. The apparently complex conversations recorded
in Speke's account must therefore be taken with a large pinch of salt.

However, in spite of his objections to sick visitors, the King, on hearing of Grant's
predicament, made arrangements to have him brought to Buganda. A party of 40 carriers,
headed by an officer, was sent to Rumanika's territory. They had been instructed to bring
the sick man and would brook no delay. On 14th April 1862, poor Captain Grant
was unceremoniously bundled onto a wicker litter and the journey started, four men
taking it in turn to carry him. Grant's usual mildness of temperament shone through.
His sole complaint was that the porters insisted on his proceeding head first, forcing
him to view the countryside through which they passed retrospectively.

Speke had been told that the outlet from the Nyanza to the north was at a place named
The Stones, some 80 km (50 miles) to the east of Mutesa's capital. The name was
a translation of the Luganda word *ejinja*, which in the course of time became corrupted
to 'Jinja', the name of the modern town near the Ripon and Owen falls. Visiting
this place had to be the crux of the expedition, but Speke had also been warned by
the *Kabaka* and his ministers, that their way further north to the Sudan would be barred
by the Banyoro, under their Muhima king, Omukama Kamrasi. There was historical
hostility between Buganda and Bunyoro, and the very fact that Speke was *persona
grata* with Mutesa, would make him an enemy in Kamrasi's eyes, while Mutesa, seeing
the prestige conferred on him by his friendship with Speke, was reluctant to let such
advantage brush off onto Kamrasi.

It was only with the utmost diplomacy and the handing of gifts originally destined
to ease their passage through new territories, that Speke and Grant were able to persuade
Mutesa to grant them safe passage out of his country. But when he did, it was in royal
style, providing them with an armed escort and a herd of 60 cattle as rations on the hoof.
Their emotional leavetaking on 7th July was marked by their host ordering the execution
of one of his wives. On 18th July their unwieldy column reached the point where
the roads divided. One route led to the east and to The Stones, while the other proceeded
to the north, to Bunyoro and then on to the Sudan. It was here that Speke took another
of the strange decisions that would mar his reputation. Their caravan was cumbersome
and while Mutesa's escort remained with them, although scarcely under their command,
it was essential that their own (non-Baganda) men and their remaining goods should
reach Kamrasi's capital, at Masindi, safely. Their goal was about 160 km (100 miles)
to the north-west and there could be no question of taking the whole unmanageable
column, cattle and all, 80 km (50 miles) in the wrong direction to The Stones and
then reversing it. A decision had to be made, and Speke did. This is how he describes
his reasoning in his journal: '…it appeared all important to communicate quickly with
Petherick, and as Grant's leg was considered too weak for travelling fast, we took counsel
together and altered our plans. I arranged that Grant should go to Kamrasi's direct with
the property, cattle and women, taking my letters and a map for immediate despatch
to Petherick at Gani, whilst I should go up the river to its source or exit from the lake,
and come down, navigating as far as practicable.'

Later on in England the anti-Speke lobby picked on this decision as a perfect example of
his 'perfidy'. Had he not deliberately contrived to ensure that to him alone should accrue
the title of discoverer of the Nile source? But these were armchair critics: anyone with
experience of that kind of terrain and of Africa will understand that, without
determination and even sometimes a touch of ruthlessness on the part of the leader of
the party, there would have been little chance of progress. For Grant to attempt to follow
Speke to the source in his poor state of health, would have spelt the end of the expedition.
Similarly, if one of them had not been in charge of the caravan, it would have had little
chance of ever reaching Kamrasi's kingdom. It has been suggested that the nobly
subservient Grant was too compliant. Whether or not this was the case, I can do no more
than quote his own words: 'Speke asked me whether I was able to make a flying march
of it along with him, while the baggage might be sent on towards Unyoro. At that time
I was positively unable to walk 20 miles [32 km] a day…I therefore yielded reluctantly

*Opposite: Speke's first view of the Stones, looking south towards Lake Victoria, showing
the cascade that would later be named the Ripon Falls and that, for a long time, would be
regarded as the definitive source of the Nile.*
*Overleaf: The Ripon Falls, or rather the swirl of water, past a giant fig tree, that is all that
remains of Mutesa's Stones, following the construction of the Owen Falls Dam.*

to the necessity of our parting; and I am anxious to be explicit on this point, as some
have hastily inferred that my companion did not wish me to share in the gratification
of seeing the river. Nothing could be more contrary to the fact. My state of health alone
prevented me from accompanying Speke.'

Their point of parting was only about 32 km (20 miles) west of a place on the Nile that
Speke calls Urondogani, which he reached in three days. This was the first sight Speke
ever had of the river to which he had given his heart and he was deeply impressed by
its beauty and majesty. He describes it as 'a magnificent stream, from 600 to 700 yards
wide [550 to 690 m], dotted with islets and rocks.' Turning south towards the lake,
through difficult country, he arrived at The Stones, seven days later, on 28th July 1862.
A cascade of water a mere 3.70 m (12 ft) in height, but which is the very lip of
the Nyanza, poured over a reef of rocky islands. This waterfall, under the name of Ripon
Falls, was to become accepted as the definitive source of the Nile. (But, of course,
and unknown to Speke at the time, the ultimate sources were still many hundreds
of miles to the south.)

It is one of the perversities of the Nile that at this strategic spot, one has no proper view
of the lake. The falls are at the inland limit of a complicated gulf (absurdly named
Napoleon – not even after the great Emperor – but after his inconsequential nephew,
Napoleon III). From Speke's viewpoint, one only commands a pleasing, but landlocked

sheet of water. Nonetheless, the falls provided a most engaging sight. Speke describes the roaring waters, some 370 to 450 m (400 to 500 yards) wide; the leaping passenger fish (barbel); the fishermen perched dangerously on the rocks; the hippos and crocodiles; the canoes serving as ferries; the pretty shores with grassy hills, tree-filled ravines, gardens and herds of cattle. He was enchanted. 'It was a sight that attracted one to it for hours…as interesting a picture as one could wish to see…I felt as if I only wanted a wife and family, garden and yacht, rifle and rod, to make me happy for life, so charming was the place.' For Speke, this was a rare reference to womanhood and he concludes his purple passage by saying that 'The expedition had now performed its functions; I saw that old Father Nile without any doubt rises in the Victoria Nyanza.'

My own description of the place, written 80 years later in 1943, differs little from his. But, alas, I was amongst the last to contemplate this scene. Soon afterwards the construction of the Owen Falls Dam caused the submersion of Speke's waterfalls: only a swirl of water, past a giant fig tree on a rocky islet, now indicates where Mutesa's Stones used to lie, and the exhilaration has been taken from the place, especially as the area has been blighted by the sprawl of Jinja township.

Speke spent three days at this lovely place and then retraced his steps, re-occupying his old camp at Urondogani, where he was held up by difficulties in obtaining a fleet of five decrepit canoes for his journey downstream. On 13th August the party set off, carried along by the increasingly placid river, that was now taking on the character of a lake. They were in fact approaching Lake Kioga, the great complex of swamp and open water that comprises the second Sudd reservoir of the Nile, but Speke was unaware of this. His crossing was now disputed by hostile Banyoro and after a minor engagement (I believe this to be the only occasion, on both his journeys, when Speke had recourse to firearms to secure passage), he had no option but to disembark and proceed on foot. Thus, he was denied the new discovery, and also the possibility of *proving* the continuity of the river. Nonetheless, and with his usual confidence, he named it the Somerset Nile, later to be renamed the Victoria Nile.

Meanwhile, Grant and the mainland column had been kept waiting by Kamrasi, the *Omukama* of Bunyoro. For some three weeks and, even after Speke's return, the suspicious King continued to keep them at arm's length. They found Bunyoro a less pleasing countryside than that of Buganda: flat, with only a few isolated hills and endless miles of small-tree woodland and tall coarse grass, often swampy. On the banks of the Kafu River, which is a major swamp drain and effluent of the Nile at the western extremity of Lake Kyoga, they came to Kamrasi's current capital village, a cluster of reed houses; but even then he played hard to get. Finally, when they met face to face on 18th of September, Kamrasi was unforthcoming and dismissive.

Kamrasi was closer to the concept of a Hima shepherd king than either Rumanika or Mutesa. His interest was centred on his great herds. Later, it was reported that his son and successor, Kabarega, personally owned 20,000 heads of cattle and 10,000 sheep. The cattle were herded in 20 different districts and each herd was of matching colour. A special herd of white long-horns, with necklets of small iron bells were kraaled within the royal enclosure at night, where they were carefully groomed and their ticks removed by hand. Their milk was for the royal household only: indeed the very title – *Omukama* – means 'milker'. There was an elaborate folk cult related to milk and a complex range of taboos as to who should do the milking, the vessels to be used and the handling of the milk. 'Crime' and 'sickness' merged into the recognition of actions that might indispose the animals or dry up their milk – shades of Samuel Butler's Utopian satire, *Erewhon*.

When Speke met Kamrasi, the latter had some 30 sisters. None of them were allowed to marry (thereby avoiding some of the conflicts of succession), they were compelled to live and die in his palace as virgins, their main occupation being the consumption of milk, which made them so fat that they were unable to walk. It took eight men to lift one of them on to a litter, and their transport provided a major problem when the exigencies of war dictated flight.

Compared with Mutesa, Kamrasi was unsophisticated. Nonetheless, he governed his kingdom without quite the same degree of brutality. Speke commented that he was of a milder disposition than Mutesa. Certainly there were individual sacrificial killings, but not the mass slaughters of Buganda. Kamrasi was even more grasping than Mutesa, however, keeping them as forced guests for three months, while stripping them of most of their remaining possessions.

In return, the *Omukama* presented them with a supply of high-quality white salt, the traditional peace offering of the Banyoro. When they enquired about its provenance, he told them that it was made on the shores of a great lake, the Lutanzige (roughly, 'the locust trap') which lay many days march to the west. Speke tried to persuade Kamrasi to allow them to visit the lake, but this was quite contrary to the King's intentions, and the request had to be abandonned.

At last, at the cost of shedding almost every remnant of their possessions, the expedition got away by canoe, down the reedy Kafu and then followed the Nile for about 80 km (50 miles), until they were obliged to disembark on the right-hand bank, as they came within earshot of the lengthy Karuma Falls.

Overleaf: The Gulf of Napoleon, near the Ripon Falls
Pages 62-63: Sunset over the Victoria Nile

If, from this point, they had followed the river westwards, they would not only have discovered the Murchison Falls and the Lutanzige (later to be called Lake Albert and then Lake Mobutu), but they would have avoided the scepticism of home-based geographers, who were able to object that they had not proved any actual connection between the river that flowed out of Lake Victoria and the White Nile of the Sudan. But both men were now at the limits of the humanly possible: physically and mentally exhausted, they took the most direct route towards Gondokoro, still some 320 km (200 miles) to the north. They actually touched the great river at two points near the confluence of the Aswa River, approximately in the region of the modern Uganda-Sudan border, but they had no means to prove that this body of water was in fact the Nile.

Above: *Speke and Grant at Kamrasi's palace, explaining the Bible to the King*

The Quarrel

The account of Speke's immense contribution to the Western world's conception of Central Africa ends with the arrival of the two friends on the fringe of the known world of the Sudan. For many years, however, Speke's discovery was to be questioned by his detractors and even by many of his friends, and it must be admitted that Speke was partly responsible for this lack of confidence in his extraordinary achievement. One such friend was Samuel Baker, and in terms of famous meetings in Africa, that of Speke and Baker at Gondokoro must rank second only to that of Livingstone and Stanley on the shores of Lake Tanganyika, nine years later.

Gondokoro (the nearest modern town is Lado) was the White Nile's terminal landing place, dictated by the Fola cataracts to the south, which prevented further navigation. It was here that the two travellers – Speke and Grant – expected to meet up with Petherick, his boats and supplies, although the Consul had not committed to be there in person. But, as mentioned before, the rendezvous had been arranged for over a year earlier, in November 1861, and, failing that, not later than June 1862. It was now early 1863 and yet Speke appears to have been convinced that Petherick would have waited for him indefinitely, and in person, at Gondokoro. It is remarkable enough that the promised boats and supplies were indeed waiting but, not surprisingly, there was no sign of Petherick himself.

Instead of him, Speke was surprised to recognise an old acquaintance, Samuel Baker, who was there with his wife Florence and a well-provisioned expedition, organised to search for the overdue travellers, as well as to explore the river to the south. The rapport was instant and the Bakers provided Speke and Grant with lordly hospitality, installing them aboard the comfortable *Kathleen*, the Pethericks' personal *dahabyeh* (river yacht). But at the same time as Speke triumphed in this felicitous outcome of their two-and-a-half years' endeavour, his mind was clouded by a dark vindictiveness – one can only think of it as pathological – against the absent Petherick. In fact, the Pethericks arrived only five days later, on 20th February – an amazingly successful rendezvous, bearing in mind that Speke was well over a year late!

John Petherick and his bride, Kathleen, had returned from England to Khartoum in October 1861 and, straightaway, as arranged, they dispatched the two boats along with their senior agent, Abdil Majid, together with a party of 70 men. These were instructed, not only to put the boats in place at Gondokoro, but to search for the explorers to the south. The Pethericks followed later, but dreadfully heavy rains flooded the countryside, blocking the passageways through the Sudd and seriously disrupting the journey: 'As far as the eye can see, in that land of misery and malaria, all is wretchedness,' wrote Petherick. By the beginning of July, they were forced to abandon the direct Bahr-el-jebel route and turn far to the west, then proceeding overland, parallel to the main Nile, before turning east again to Gondokoro. Abdil Majid, however, was more successful and had reached Gondokoro a month earlier, with the boats, the supplies and the *Kathleen*.

Long before the Pethericks reached Gondokoro, rumours of their deaths had spread to Khartoum and England. The Royal Geographical Society now realised that their plan to relieve Speke and Grant by sending boats and supplies via Petherick, might come to nothing. However, they knew that for the previous two years, Samuel Baker had been travelling in the eastern Sudan, exploring the Nile affluents from Abyssinia. When Baker and his wife reached Khartoum in the middle of 1862, they found that a request from the Society to mount a back-up relief expedition was waiting for them. With tremendous energy the Bakers were able to force the Sudd passage and reach Gondokoro on 2nd February 1863, where they found Petherick's boats but no reports of his or of Speke's whereabouts.

Eventually, when Speke and Grant walked into Gondokoro, 13 days later, it was the Bakers they met and not the Pethericks. The hapless couple would, as a result, earn themselves the most heartless snub in the history of African exploration, when they themselves reached Gondokoro. John Petherick describes the meeting: 'Stepping ashore at Gondokoro, we found not only Baker...but to our most agreeable surprise, also Captains Speke and Grant in possession of our dahabyeh, the *Kathleen*. Instead however of the cordial greetings I had anticipated from the ardently sought and now successful travellers, we were met with a coolness and a positive refusal to partake of more of our stores or assistance than would satisfy their most urgent requirements...Without any intimation of his reasons for doing so, Speke immediately removed his effects from the *Kathleen* and in reply to my earnest solicitations that he should retain possession of her...coolly replied "I do not wish to recognise the succour dodge".' Speke added that his good friend Baker had offered to supply all his needs and that he preferred to travel down to Khartoum in Baker's boat.

Speke's boorish manners seemed to stem from a neurotic fantasy that Petherick had betrayed him by attending to his commercial affairs at the expense of those of the expedition. The fact that Petherick had fulfilled his contract, in the letter as well as the spirit, keeping in mind Speke's own suggestion, that commerce and exploration should be advantageously combined, was lost on Speke. The Pethericks at once realised the awkward position in which they had been placed: by refusing their help Speke would be able to claim – as indeed he did – that they had defaulted on their contract with the Society, also implying that the £1,000 of sponsorship money had been improperly used.

John Petherick's account of these distressing events did not appear until six years later, when his book, *Travels in Central Africa (Vol. II)*, was published in 1869, five years after Speke's death. Petherick's account, though reproachful, is also muted. Not so the letter written at the time by his wife, Kathleen, to her sister, when news reached them of the malicious way in which Speke reported the affair after his return to England. All her wifely heartbreak and loyalty is revealed: 'Is it possible that Speke can have so acted? It seems incredible that he should impugn the honour and integrity of Petherick: my heart is filled with bitterness...he not to say that everything we had was placed at his disposal...They dined with us; and a tremendous ham which we had brought out from England was cooked. During dinner I endeavoured to prevail upon Speke to accept our aid, but he drawlingly replied, "I do not wish to recognise the succour dodge." The rest of the conversation I am not well enough to repeat.'

Poor Kathleen and her precious boiled ham! In the annals of African travel some famous meetings and dinner parties have been described, but for sheer agony, can any compare with the frosty atmosphere of that evening aboard the *Kathleen*, sitting under the tropical stars, in the stifling mosquito-infested air of the Nile. In his narrative, Speke makes almost no mention of either Kathleen or Florence: such was his asexuality, one feels, that he was entirely contemptuous of the presence of two attractive young women in the macho world of the Nile sources.

So, the three parties separated: Speke and Grant down the Nile and then on to England and the heady atmosphere of the Royal Geographical Society; the Bakers heading south to seek the new lake – the Lutanzige – the putative second great basin of the Nile, leaving the wounded Pethericks in the infernal limboland of Gondokoro.

One might have thought that the Pethericks' cup of bitterness was full to overflowing, but worse was to come. In England, Speke, in his home town of Taunton, made a thinly disguised attack on Petherick, referring to 'men in authority from our own government who are engaged with native kings in the diabolical slave trade.' Ironically, even as Speke was making this address, his friend, Samuel Baker, was perforce 'engaging with native slaving kings,' as the only way in which he could move his expedition south.

There are many biographies of Burton, but only two of Speke. Byron Farwell, in his 1963 portrait, expresses the opinion that 'The more one learns of Speke's character, the less wholesome it is revealed. It is difficult to escape the conclusion that the discoverer of the major source of the Nile and the largest lake in Africa was a cad.' Alexander Maitland, in his equally excellent 1971 biography of Speke, offers an apologium: 'Speke was not the guilty "cad" that several writers would have us believe. Rather he was trusting, easily swayed by charm, and possessed of that comb of vanity which, if stroked gently and often, would so deprive him of all good judgement that he would

temporarily forsake the path of reason for others alien and even quite disastrous.'
But isn't this statement a rather convoluted way of saying that, at times, Speke could
behave like a cad?

Maitland's comment refers to Speke's behaviour with Burton. He passes no comment on
Speke's gratuitous attack on Petherick: what 'comb of vanity' could excuse this far worse
behaviour? Far worse, because Burton was well able to give as good as he got, while
the more humble Pethericks found their reputation and livelihood destroyed. The acid test
for a gentleman, was his behaviour towards those who might be considered below him
in the social pecking order. Whatever the fine definition of a cad might be, Speke's
behaviour to the Pethericks was disgraceful for a gentleman, and so was Baker's who
did not protest at Speke's behaviour. The affair greatly detracts from the reputation
of each and even Grant cannot be exonerated totally from a charge of sins of omission.
Indeed, later on in Britain, he unequivocally took Speke's side. As for the Royal
Geographical Society, present-day Fellows can only deplore its meanness of spirit.

If anything can be said in defence of Speke's conduct, it is that his mind may have been
affected by a condition I have noticed in myself and in others and which I would call:
'post-safari neurosis'. It can also be observed in mountaineers, after their descent from
the summit; in sailors returning from long ocean voyages; and in soldiers, recently
out from action. The sudden change of pace and the drop of adrenaline cause a strange
deflation of the spirits. Burton himself seems to have experienced it, following his return
to Zanzibar with Speke. He summed it up at the time: 'the excitement of travel
was succeeded by utter depression of mind and body.'

At such times the mind of the traveller becomes obsessed with the idea that only *he* can
possibly know what he went through. This attitude produces a certain contempt for those
who did not share his adventures. In the case of Speke and the Pethericks, it is ironical
that the former should be so dismissive of people who almost lost their lives trying
to fulfil their promise and keep up their appointment with him. As Henry Morton Stanley
was to put it a quarter of a century later: '…no African traveller ought to be judged
during the first year of his return. He is so full of his own reflections…his nerves are
not uniformly strung and his mind harks back to the strange scenes he has just left.'
Certainly, one needs very understanding friends at such a time!

The Speke and Burton controversy, ie the Victoria system versus the Tanganyika-Albert
hypothesis, was to run and run, but Speke's triumphalist telegram from Khartoum,
crowing that 'The Nile is settled' was received joyfully enough in Britain. At first, on
his return, Speke was welcomed unconditionally as the discoverer of the definitive source
of the Nile, but it was not long before the acclaims began to cool. The argument steadily
grew in strength that he had failed to show convincingly that the Nyanza was a single

entity, or that the river that flowed over the Ripon Falls was necessarily anything to do with the Nile. Livingstone had reasons for disagreeing with him, albeit he did so courteously. But, in the case of Burton, there was to be no question of courtesy. Still embittered by Speke's behaviour, he allowed his judgement to become clouded by personal enmity. He wrote to the Secretary of the Royal Geographical Society: 'I don't want to have any further private or indirect communication with Speke.' He was incensed by the publication of Speke's two books, and this prompted him to resurrect the Lake-Tanganyika theory and set about the demolition of Speke's claims with vindictive energy.

He had a point: what did Speke's discoveries amount to? In 1859 he had glimpsed a modestly sized lake and, in 1862, an even smaller one, some 500 km (200 miles) to the north. He had made no effort, however, to demonstrate a tangible link between the two. He had found an outlet from this second lake, but failed to prove its continuity with the already known White Nile. Burton, with his intellectual superiority, might have been expected to remain rational, instead of which he allowed himself to be supported by the academic geographer, James McQueen. In a childish, but scurrilous, indeed libellous review of Speke's *Journal of the Discovery of the Source of the Nile (1864)*, McQueen set out, not only to deride and demolish Speke's achievements, but also his character, questioning his motives and his morals in dealing with Africans. I said that there is something childish in McQueen's attempts at character assassination and it is shown in his ponderous sarcasms. As a final dart of derision, he suggests that, doubtless, one day there would be a Ripon Falls hotel and a railway bringing tourists. This statement, must surely haunt him for, in 1943, I stayed at a pleasant hotel, a short walk from the falls and, of course, I had travelled to Uganda on the railway. Life is full of these little ironies.

Burton was so blinded by antagonism that he allowed McQueen's review to appear as part of a short co-authored work, *The Nile Basin*, published in 1864. In this, Burton claims Lake Tanganyika to be the great western reservoir mentioned by Ptolemy and the ancients, and draining into the Lutanzige. Speke's Nyanza, on the other hand, he demotes to a maze of swamps and small lakes, fed by minor rivers. Ill-advisedly, Burton endorsed the opinions of the Reverend Thomas Wakefield, who had joined the Church Missionary Society, at Mombasa, in 1861. Although Wakefield scarcely left the coast, Burton characteristically set reliance on his philologically convoluted arguments about reported place names (the pitfall of many an African geographer). He asserts that Wakefield's researches led 'to a certainty...to the conclusion that the area of 29,000 square geographical miles assigned to the so-called Victoria Nyanza contains at least four and probably a greater number of separate waters; that it is in fact, not a lake, but a Lake Region.' The book – *The Nile Basin* – can be recommended as an amusing read, of little use to the geographer, but of great interest to the student of Victorian manners. The obvious way to solve the question – another expedition – does not, however, seem

to have been considered. During this summer of 1864, Speke made more than one visit
to Paris, and the possibility of an Anglo-French, Trans-African scheme, designed 'to open
up Africa,' was being canvassed. This 'opening up of Africa' entailed the propagation
of the Christian faith, as well as geographical exploration. Meanwhile, the resources
of the Royal Geographical Society were still being squandered to support more of
Dr Livingstone's inconclusive wanderings to the south.

The controversy could not continue to inflate without exploding. In keeping with
the traditions of the age, a verbal duel was called for. Customarily, the Geographical
Society held its annual meeting in conjunction with the British Association for
the Advancement of Science. In the late summer of 1864 it was to be held at Bath,
a city not far from the country estate of Speke's uncle at Neston Park. A debate
was arranged, to be led by the main antagonists, Speke and Burton and it was expected
that the dispute would be brought to a head. Livingstone himself was to take part,
but not Grant, who was in Scotland writing his book, nor Baker, who had not
yet returned from his travels. Speke by now was almost *persona non grata* with
the Society, having deliberately defaulted on his obligation to supply them with a detailed
paper on his discoveries for their proceedings, in favour of rushing his book out in order
to catch the Christmas trade.

Burton attended the Bath meeting with his loyal wife, Isabel. Speke had no such support,
but he stayed with his uncle and relaxed in the way he liked best – rough shooting.
The debate was scheduled for 16th September, in the Hall of the Mineral Water Hospital.
There was an earlier meeting on the morning of the 15th at which Speke and Burton
cut each other icily. Speke left abruptly for Neston where, in the afternoon, he went
out shooting with his cousin George and the gamekeeper. He was using a double-barrelled
Lancaster breech loader, a gun that required cocking, but had no safety guard for
the two triggers. The men were separated, when George Fuller heard a single shot.
Looking back, he saw Speke, who had been crossing a low stone wall, collapse.
On reaching him, he found that one barrel had discharged into Speke's side: he was dead
within a quarter of an hour.

An inquest held next day produced a verdict of accidental death. Inevitably, there was a
rumour that Speke, under mental strain, might have taken his own life. For a while,
the lion-hearted survivor of so many close encounters with death seemed to have left
the world with an enigma. But there was no enigma. The facts spoke for themselves:
the dimensions of the gun, the discharge of the further of the two triggers, and the entry
point of the shot, made it a practical impossibility for Speke to have killed himself
intentionally. Soon, the full details were reported in *The Times*.

In the end, Speke's findings were vindicated and he would have his triumph, although it took another decade. Furthermore this late recognition did not come through the efforts of the Royal Geographical Society, but through the initiative of two newspapers and of Stanley's tour de force. McQueen, nonentity that he was, disappeared from the scene. But what of Burton? Only the closest scrutiny of the literature reveals his eventual bitter realisation that he had been the real victim of this tragedy of self-inflicted wounds – the victim of his own intellectual arrogance.

There is a curiously morbid postscript to this story. Burton, in his massive book, *Zanzibar*, published in 1872, after the manuscript had lain forgotten for eight years, apparently lost in a strong box in India, mentions that the sculptor, Edgar Papworth, had taken a death mask of Speke. When Isabel and Richard Burton visited his studio to view the almost completed clay model, the artist, explaining that he had not known Speke while he was alive, asked for Burton's comments. Burton, who had once dabbled in sculpture, took up the artist's stylus and, with a few confident strokes, completed the likeness.

Soon after, ostensibly Isabel Burton – but surely Richard himself – wrote a tediously long poem inspired by the sculpture. It was published under Isabel's name, in *Fraser's Magazine* and was reproduced by Burton in his *Zanzibar* book. Sorrowfully, the poem explores the relationship between the two men and the following extract gives us the sole indication that Burton may have experienced some regrets:

'And our objects fated to disagree,
What way went I, and what way went he?
Yet we were comrades for years and years,
And endured in its troth our companionship
Through a life of chances, of hopes and fears;
Nor a word of harshness e'er passed the lip,
Nor a thought unkind dwelt in either heart,
Till we chanced – by what chance did it hap? – to part.'

Not 'a word of harshness…Nor a thought unkind?' Perhaps these lines, at least, were Isabel's, since she had devoted her life, to the protection of her husband's image.

As for Speke, his plain obelisk of red Scottish granite still stands in Kensington Gardens, not far from the modern headquarters of the Royal Society he had snubbed. Originally, the plaque was terse to the point of obscurity, bearing the single word 'AFRICA'. In 1995, however, and not without a resurgence of the Burton controversy, the Friends of Hyde Park and Kensington Gardens added a fuller explanatory plaque. But, perhaps the most penetrating epitaph comes from Speke's biographer, Alexander Maitland: 'May he be forgiven if he foresaw only the goodness and prosperity and not the evil and concomitant decay which would result from the breaking open of Africa's dark core.'

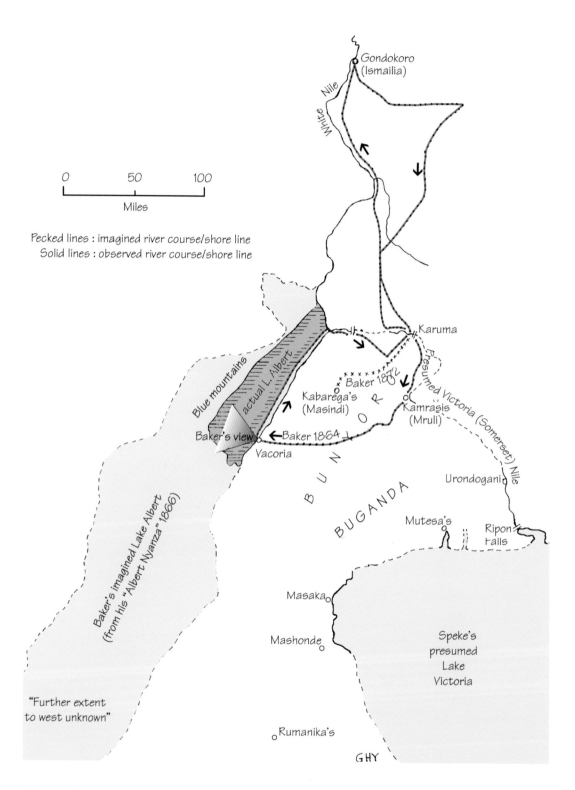

Gondokoro
(Ismailia)

White Nile

0   50   100
Miles

Pecked lines : imagined river course/shore line
Solid lines : observed river course/shore line

Karuma

Presumed Victoria (Somerset) Nile

Baker 1872

Blue mountains

actual L. Albert

Kabarega's
(Masindi)

Kamrasis
(Mruli)

Baker's view

Baker 1864

Vacoria

B U N O R

BUGANDA

Urondogani

Baker's imagined Lake Albert
(from his "Albert Nyanza" 1866)

Mutesa's

Ripon
Falls

Masaka

Mashonde

Speke's
presumed
Lake
Victoria

"Further extent
to west unknown"

Rumanika's

GHY

Above: *The map shows the route followed by the Bakers in 1864 and the place where they first viewed Lake Albert. It indicates the extent of Baker's imagined Albert Nyanza, compared with the size of the actual Lake Albert. The map also shows Speke's speculative shoreline of Lake Victoria.*

The False Lake

Samuel Baker was another representative of the breed of Victorian upper class eccentrics whose lives were dictated by their sense of adventure and of patriotic endeavour. He was an Englishman who, when in Scotland, and by permission of the Duke, would don the Atholl tartan. He is most remembered for his three splendid books about his travels in the Nile basin between 1861 and 1873, and for his engaging young Transylvanian partner, Florence, whether mistress or wife, who shared his adventures so courageously. He was widely travelled, an adventurous sportsman and the personification of the Victorian man of talent and independent means.

On the death of his first wife, Baker entrusted his four daughters to one of his sisters' care and set out on an-open-ended sporting journey to the Danube basin, which was then a disputed region between the Austro-Hungarian and the Ottoman empires. Slavery still flourished under Turkish rule and, one day in 1858, in the fortress town of Widdin, in modern-day Bulgaria, Baker looked in at the auction. As the bidding proceeded, his eye fell upon a young girl with golden hair. He found himself bidding and she became his, for an undisclosed sum of Turkish lira. Her name was Florence Finnian. She was a German-speaking Hungarian Roman Catholic, the only one of her family to have survived a massacre during the Transylvanian uprising of 1848. Samuel was 38, she was a mere 17.

Whether Baker was instantly infatuated, we do not know, but instead of returning to England, he took on a local railway construction contract and, in due course, having gone through an unexplained form of ceremony, set up house with Florence as his wife. Within two years, they were in Africa. They were made for each other. She was as tough as she was gentle, courageous as she was frail, his ideal companion and an unfailingly loyal supporter, amidst all the hardships and tribulations they would encounter. Baker's books are buoyant and frank, if self-opinionated, but they owe a good deal of their charm to the loving way in which he refers to Florence. Her empathy touched all around her. Whatever reservations the local peoples might feel against her overbearing husband, they all fell under her spell. This extraordinary woman became known as *Myadue*, the Morning Star, or its equivalent *Nyadwe*, Daughter of the Moon. Of Samuel's many tributes to her, this is perhaps the most telling. He describes her as: 'possessing a share of sang froid admirably adapted to African travel, Mrs Baker was not a screamer, and never even whispered in the moment of danger.' She certainly needed 'sang froid', she once came out of a week-long coma to find the men digging her grave! This was no Cook's tour.

Above: This portrait of Florence, the future Lady Baker, was taken in Paris when she was aged 24. She would soon become introduced to fashionable London.

Above: *Samuel Baker in 1865. He wears the 'suit' he designed to wear during the expedition and which was made up by the faithful Florence.*

Baker had started his journey in 1861, taking his time, learning Arabic and the art of Nile travel. Now at Gondokoro, in a meeting that was the worthy precursor of the famous one between Stanley and Dr Livingstone, he met Speke who had forestalled him at the source. But the latter, and one must allow that this was generous, gave the Bakers a copy of his map on which was pencilled an as yet speculative route to the great western lake, the Lutanzige. Baker saw at once that finding this new lake, at least, would be a worthy consolation prize – and who was to say which of the lakes would turn out to be the more important reservoir of the Nile? The size of Lake Victoria could still only be guessed at, while even Lake Tanganyika had not been totally eliminated. Might there not be a river flowing between the Tanganyika and the Lutanzige that would turn out to be the main Nile, thus marginalizing Speke's Nyanza?

Following the rendezvous at Gondokoro the Bakers set out southwards in March 1863, intending to retrace Speke's steps to King Kamrasi's palace in Bunyoro. But the tribes, through whose regions they had to pass, notably the Bari, were up in arms against the iniquitous slave traders and any stranger was likely to be taken for one. Baker had, perforce, to compromise with his principles and accept the protection of the slaving columns. It took them nine months to reach Kamrasi's frontier, at the Karuma Falls, on the Victoria Nile. By January 1864, when Baker and his wife at last reached Kamrasi's court, they were both seriously weakened by fever. Unknown to them, the *Omukama* with whom they treated, was in fact a substitute – Kamrasi's brother – the real *Omukama* fearing bewitchment. For whatever reasons, they were subjected to maddening delays, deceit and cupidity, although this may be just another way of describing Banyoro caution in admitting strangers to their country. In February, driven to despair, Baker demanded guides and the right of passage to the Lutanzige, the *Omukama* conceded at last on condition that Florence was left behind as part of the royal household! Baker drew his pistol and held it to the man's chest, while Florence rose from her sick bed and, in graphic terms, told the *Omukama*, or his double, what she thought of his plan: 'a speech in Arabic with a countenance almost as amiable as Medusa.' The man wisely withdrew his proposition and allowed them to set off the next day.

The journey of about 160 km (100 miles) to the southwest took them through the swamps of the Kafu river system. Even with a Landrover, this is difficult and depressing terrain. For the Bakers it was a nightmare, each of them successively coming close to death. After eleven marches, the land rose a little, and on higher ground, they entered the Bugoma forest, which is still one of Uganda's finest natural forests. On the morning of 14th March 1864, they ascended a gentle rise and then: 'The glory of our prize burst suddenly upon me. There, like a sea of quicksilver, lay far beneath the grand expanse of water – a boundless sea horizon on the south and south-west, glittering in the noonday sun; and on the west, at fifty or sixty miles [80 or 95 km] distance, blue mountains rose from the bosom of the lake to a height of about 7000 feet [over 2,000 m] above its level.'

Baker's vision differed little from mine, when I first reached the escarpment edge, nearly 80 years later. I had the advantage of a map, but the Bakers, unfortunately if understandably, allowed themselves to be carried away by euphoria. There was no sea horizon to the south, only the ever-present haze that conceals the low-lying shore and, far beyond, the snow-capped Rwenzori mountain range. The distance across the sea to what he called the 'Blue Mountains', was scarcely 50 km (30 miles), and their height above the surface of the water was less than 1,500 m (5,000 ft). It was the supposed sea horizon to the south that would later cause him so much embarrassment. In his eagerness to make his source of the Nile more important than the one found by Speke, he allowed himself to elaborate on native reports of yet other lakes further south: Lake Edward and Lake Kivu, which no European had yet seen. Knowing, and evidently hearing nothing of the great mountain mass in between, he extended the Lutanzige (now christened Lake Albert), to include the waters of Edward and Kivu, creating an imaginary huge Nyanza Lake that far surpassed Speke's Lake Victoria. Only years later, was it established that Baker had actually been close to the southernmost limits of a lake of only second-class dimensions by African standards, and that Lake Edward was indeed connected to Lake Albert by the Semliki River.

Putting this aside, we must simply rejoice with the man and the girl at the moment of their discovery. Their lake lay in a huge rift trench, 534 m (1,750 ft) below them. It is a sight that never failed to fill me with wonder, although there is something awsome about it that gives the spectator a feeling of unease. There is little comforting evidence of humanity: the tints of the waters are often the dully luminescent greys of lead and mercury. Although the escarpment walls have some vegetation, wherever the steep gradients allow, there is a sense of sterility, and one descends into the trough with a feeling of oppression, only to be overwhelmed by the stagnant heat. Colonel Gordon, whose life ended tragically at the Siege of Khartoum 20 years later, left a telling description of his visit to the lake by the first steamer: 'What a wilderness is up here, not a sound to be heard and all so lifeless and apparently miserable.'

So steep is the rocky escarpment at the point where the Bakers' guides led them down to the shore, that there is, to this day, only one practicable passage: a descent so narrow that each person is compelled to use certain hand- and foot-holds. Baker describes the descent as 'steep and dangerous'. There is no serious danger but, as a result of the rubbing of thousands of hands and feet over the centuries, as the sparse residents of the narrow shore traded their only product – dried fish – for firewood and other necessaries from the tops, the rock-holds have in places become polished. In 1991, I set out deliberately to follow the Bakers' path. As the grey sea below lit up like a fire

Overleaf: The western face of Mount Stanley in the Rwenzori mountain range, seen from Mount Wasumaweso in Zaire.

opal with the awakening of a new African day, I found myself using the ancient steps, cautiously, hand and foot, electrified with the thrill that these were the actual holds touched by Samuel and his beautiful Florence.

Most of the cliffs fall so steeply that there is neither beach nor ground for human beings to stand on. But at the points where the mountain torrents fall, alluvial fans have formed, and such is the case at Vacovia (Bakovia), the rather unusual name that Baker gave to the present fishing village of Buhuka. One crosses a mile of sparse grassland and bushes – a near desert in the dry season – through a miserable scatter of grass huts, before reaching the water's edge where the canoes are drawn up amongst scavenging marabou storks and pelicans. The Bakers were sick and weary: Samuel describes Florence as '... pale and exhausted – a wreck upon the shores of the great Albert Lake that we had so far striven to reach.' But nothing could diminish their joy as they 'rushed into the lake and, thirsty with heat and fatigue, with a heart full of gratitude...drank deeply from the sources of the Nile.'

Although mistaken about the actual size of Lake Albert, Baker was correct in his conclusions about its function: this was indeed another great basin of the Nile: 'every drop of water...that drained central Africa towards the north' must pass through this lake: it was indeed the final mediator of the perennial flow of the White Nile.

Baker had sent his main party, together with their riding oxen, overland to Magungo, at the north end of the lake. He now embarked with his few remaining companions in dugout canoes for a coasting voyage northwards. It took them 13 storm-tossed days to reach Magungo, by which time the lake had narrowed to only 6 to 8 km (4 to 5 miles). From there, through a confusing delta of reeds, they were able to paddle eastwards up the incoming Victoria Nile. I am familiar with this spot: after about 16 km (10 miles), the reeds are left behind and the traveller finds himself in the well defined channel of a great river, bordered by forest-clad cliffs – a gloriously wild world given over to hippos, crocodiles and giant monitor lizards. After the Bakers had travelled just under 16 km (18 miles) from the lake, they became aware of a thunderous roar and the current became stronger and spume-flecked. They were astonished by the population of crocodiles: 'they lay like logs of timber close together.' Rounding a bend, a magnificent sight burst upon them: 'On either side of the river were beautiful wooded cliffs rising abruptly to a height of about 300 feet [90 m]; rocks were jutting out from the intensely green foliage: and rushing through the gap that cleft the rock exactly before us, the river, contracted from a grand stream, was pent up in a narrow gorge of scarcely fifty yards [45 m] in width; roaring furiously through the rock-bound pass, it plunged into a dark abyss below. The fall of water was snow white, which had a superb effect as it contrasted with the dark cliffs that walled the river, while the graceful palms of the tropics and the wild plantains perfected the beauty of the view. This was the greatest waterfall of the Nile, and in honour of the distinguished President of the Royal Geographical Society, I named it the Murchison Falls, as the most important object throughout the entire course of the river.'

Baker made a sketch of the falls from his canoe which, worked up by his publisher's engraver in England, comes near to doing justice to the splendid subject, but is not altogether accurate: his cascade is too broad and conventional (see page 84). In fact, the whole force of the Nile is crammed into a gap, considerably narrower than his 45 m (50 yards) – indeed it is a mere 9 m (10 yards) wide – but as it projects downwards into a deep cleft, it makes it difficult to get an unobstructed view.

This culmination of success did not spell the end of the Bakers' troubles, the worst was yet to come. Their riding oxen had succumbed to tsetse-borne disease. Samuel and Florence were both so weak that they had to be carried on litters and they only managed to follow the Nile upstream from the falls for a short way, before war between Kamrasi and his rebels forced them south, to camp in the sour wastes of the tall grass and

Opposite: One of the many crocodiles that are a common sight throughout the Nile basin. Campaigns of eradication in the waters of Lake Victoria, caused the Nile perch population – an introduced species with no other predator than the crocodile – to spiral out of control and to eradicate the once abundant native species of fish.

woodlands that characterise so much of Bunyoro. For several months, without quinine or other resources, they lay in misery. This place, which Baker called Kisoona (Kisuna), was still an unprepossessing wilderness when I visited it in 1991, and I can well understand their despair.

It was here that they finally discovered that the so-called 'King Kamrasi', with whom they had dealt on their way south, was an impostor. He was the *Omukama's* brother, M'Gambi, put forward by Kamrasi out of fear of being put under a spell. However, the real Kamrasi proved to be just as refractory and grasping as his double. It was only when he was distracted by a fortuitous invasion by an Arab slaving caravan from the north and by a sweep by Bagandan armies from the south, that Kamrasi was compelled to allow the Bakers to concentrate their party at the Karuma Falls and eventually to leave for the north. The couple had been held virtual prisoners for over seven months. It now took them three months through the hostile Madi country to reach Gondokoro, a year later than they had hoped originally. Hiring an Arab *dahabyeh*, they eventually reached Khartoum in May 1865 and, from there, proceeded to Cairo via the Red Sea route. In that city, Samuel was at last able to indulge his craving for Allsopps Pale Ale.

'The past appeared like a dream,' he writes on the last page of his famous book, '...Had I really come from the Nile sources? It was no dream. A witness sat before me; a face still young, but bronzed like an Arab with years of exposure to a burning sun; haggard and worn with toil and sickness, and shaded with cares now past; the devoted companion of my pilgrimage to whom I owed success and life – my wife.'

Wife, she certainly was in every real sense of the word; but neither state nor church had blessed their union. Baker must have wondered what might be the consequences of introducing this extraordinary young woman, still only 24 years old, to his upper-class family, especially to his unmarried sister Min, who had brought his children up, following his first wife's death, and to the Victorian society by whose rules they were bound. Readers, breathe freely! After a civil ceremony at the British embassy in Paris, they were publicly united at St James' church, Piccadilly, and it took little time for Florence to win the hearts of at least part of Samuel's family. Samuel Baker was knighted, but tales of Florence's colourful past still clung to her and Queen Victoria for one, refused steadfastly to receive the newly coined Lady Baker. She was indeed far from 'amused' when Samuel became a close friend of the Prince of Wales. Yet, the couple soon became the toast of London society and theirs was a long and gloriously successful marriage. The story of the Bakers' first expedition is thrilling, but truth to tell, they had not

Opposite: The Murchison Falls discovered by Samuel and Florence Baker and named by them in honour of Sir Roderick Murchison, who was the President of the Royal Geographical Society.

achieved very much. Their only discovery of significance was Lake Albert. Over-stating his case, Samuel wrote: 'The Albert Nyanza is the great basin of the Nile; the distinction between that and the Victoria Nyanza is, that the Victoria is a reservoir receiving the eastern affluents, and it becomes a starting part of the most elevated source at the point where the river issues from it at the Ripon Falls: the Albert is a reservoir not only receiving the western and southern affluents direct from the Blue Mountains, but it also receives the supply from the Victoria and from the entire equatorial basin. The Nile, as it issues from the Albert lake is the entire Nile.

'Until its birth from the Albert Lake it is not the entire Nile. A glance at the map will at once exemplify the relative value of the two great lakes...'

Transparently Samuel Baker was fishing for precedence over Speke, but the map at which we are invited to glance was a poetic speculation. Lake Albert is shown as substantially greater than a still only putative Victoria – an immense 145 km (90 mile) wide trench, extending at least two degrees south of the Equator – then disappearing off the edge of the page and entering the world of the imagination, limitlessly to the west. It is doubtful whether Baker would have dared to publish this piece of creative geography, had Speke still been alive. But he *did* publish it, two years after his friend's death, and it must have remained an embarrassment for the rest of his life.

Baker's Commission

1869 – 1873

Florence Baker had less than five years in which to acquaint herself with her adopted family and country. In 1869 the eyes of the world were on Egypt, where the Suez Canal was on the point of completion. Prior to the official opening, the Prince of Wales and Princess Alexandra (the future King Edward VII and his Queen) visited the scene, taking the Bakers with them as interpreters. At a fancy-dress ball in Cairo given by the chief architect of the canal, Ferdinand de Lesseps, the Khedive Ismail took Samuel aside and asked him to accept a four-year commission with the ranks of Pasha and Major-General. He was to lead an Egyptian expeditionary force to the south and annexe the headwaters of the Nile, ostensibly for the purpose of suppressing the slave trade. Khedive Ismail was engaged in a costly programme for the westernization of Egypt, that involved an ever-increasing indebtedness to the western nations, that put them in a position to put pressure on him over the moral issue of slavery in his dominions. Baker, and everyone else involved, knew that slavery was ingrained in the Egyptian way of life: every official was a slave owner, with the Khedive as the chief among them. But when the latter, speaking with disarming candour, announced his philanthropic initiative and that it was to be headed by such an internationally respected personality as Samuel Baker, who could do otherwise but commend it?

Baker was being only partly naive. If he questioned Ismail's real motives, he also believed that once he himself was established as ruler of the Nile springs, with the absolute powers that went with the office, he could ensure the enlightened governance of the region and the neutralisation of the slave barons. In any case, there was no question of his turning down such an attractive assignment, so suited to his own character and abilities. It would surely provide him *inter alia* with the opportunity to substantiate his claim for his greater Albert Nyanza and the ultimate Nile sources.

To be fair to Khedive Ismail, his motives were no worse than those of the western powers that in due course would scramble for this part of Africa. The main difference was that he anticipated them by two decades! Unlike the Europeans, he did at least share a land-frontier with the region into which he aspired, and therefore felt some responsibility

Opposite: This is the engraving of the Murchison Falls that appeared in Samuel Baker's book: The Albert N'yanza, Great Basin of the Nile, *published in 1866. The engraving was based on Baker's sketch and was not altogether accurate (compare with the photograph of the Falls on page 82) yet, combined with his account of the discovery, it made an enormous impression on his readers.*

for what went on in the savage lands beyond – an argument that hardly applied to people separated by thousands of miles of ocean. For him, the real aim was to encompass the Sudan, Abyssinia, eastern and central Africa within a Greater Egypt, that would control every part of the Nile catchment.

If there were powerful voices in Britain arguing quite seriously that her position in India depended on her control of the Nile valley, how much more important would this control appear to Khedive Ismail and his totally Nile-dependent state? One must understand the feelings of a people whose entire way of life relied on a running channel of water, the sources of which were indefinitely far away and entirely beyond their reach. It is not enough to accuse Khedive Ismail of a folly of aggrandisement: there was a more basic instinct for national survival behind his strategy, something that, in our time, found expression in the creation of Lake Nasser, at Aswan.

Baker was quite prepared to go along with the Khedive and, in euphoric mood, declared that it was his task 'to open a road to a great future, where the past had been all darkness and the present reckless spoilation.' There were no financial constraints, the river itself imposed the only restriction: there was a limit as to what it was practicable to move over the 4,800 km (3,000 miles) distance from the delta to equatoria. By this time, there were

many modern steamers on the lower Nile, as well as large numbers of heavy sailing vessels – *nuggars* – of a capacity of around 50 tons. A fleet of nine large steamers and 55 *nuggars* was assembled at Khartoum, while three sectional steamers and two steel lifeboats, made in Britain, were packaged for transport beyond the most southerly cataracts for service on Lake Albert. The army under Baker's command comprised 1,700 men: half of them a Sudanese regiment which, surprisingly, had seen service in Mexico under the French Marshal Bazaine; the other half was composed, in Baker's words, 'of the convicted felons of Cairo's prisons.' Armaments included three-pound rockets, 'blue light flares', and light mountain guns. The European staff, apart from Samuel and Florence, consisted of Samuel's nephew, Lieutenant Julian Baker R N, and of a dozen of British engineers and shipwrights.

At Khartoum the expeditionary force met obstruction from the officials and traders whose lives were dependent on the slave trade. Baker's writ commenced 96 km (60 miles) further south, and he lost as little time as possible in shaking off the tentacles of Egyptian rule. But he had not moved fast enough for the river: the Sudd closed in and, as the soldiers laboured for week after week, hacking a passage through the papyrus, the water level fell and they were forced to retreat downstream to Malakal, in order to await the next flood. Thanks to these delays, they did not reach Gondokoro until April 1871.

Baker renamed the place Ismailia and soon had a model headquarters for the new province laid out, raising the Egyptian flag and announcing annexation ceremonially, much to the bemusement of the natives. This was the sort of thing Samuel revelled in, but it was all froth and bubbles: within four months, they were beleaguered by the local tribes and facing starvation. While he was absent on a foray, most of Baker's army defected by commandeering boats and sailing off down the Nile. If anything, the loss of this burdensome and food-consuming mass of people was beneficial to him. Selecting some 200 loyal men, including a Praetorian guard dubbed 'The Forty Thieves' by Florence, he sailed upstream to the foot of the cataracts, at Fola. He took his steamer party overland up to Afuddo, where the Nile once more became navigable, and left the engineers to work. Samuel, Florence and Julian continued on towards Bunyoro, hearing for the first time of the death of the *Omukama* Kamrasi and of the succession of his son, Kabarega. Baker moved on quickly, reaching the Victoria Nile at his old crossing point at Foweira. He marched boldly into the wildly independent kingdom and came to Kabarega's always readily translocatable capital, at Masindi. Treating the gauche and inexperienced young *Omukama* with scorn, and without any pretence of negotiating an agreement, he proceeded to build a government residence and, on 14th May 1872, he raised the Egyptian flag, declaring the formal annexation of Bunyoro to Egypt.

Opposite: The rotting hulk of an old lake steamer. These craft would once have provided a vital lifeline for passengers and trade.

When I first visited Masindi in the 1940s, it had developed into a busy staging post on the upper Nile sector of the Cape to Cairo road, with neat bungalows, green lawns, blue-blossomed jacaranda trees and pretty gardens, all immaculate under the Union flag. It even boasted a pleasant European-style hotel, quaintly called the Railway Hotel, although there was no railway within a hundred miles! In spite of the subsequent years of abuse and neglect under anarchic independence, it is still a pretty place and the people are unassumingly nice. However, as John Beattie, in his book, *Bunyoro*, remarks, '…if there is some reserve and a touch of melancholy in their make up this should not surprise anyone who is acquainted with their history.' This makes the insufferably boorish behaviour of Baker even more embarrassing for the British reader and the fact that he was not operating as a representative of the British Empire, provides no justification.

But, in the end, his contemptuous dismissal of Kabarega proved fatal to his purpose. The young king was much more of an adversary than the incompetent delinquent described by Baker. Kabarega and his subjects were filled with a justifiable anger as the westerner's behaviour became ever more high-handed. Baker's residence turned into a besieged *laager*, increasingly hemmed in with native huts, half-concealed in the tall grass, that occluded his field of fire. Baker, realising his vulnerable position, made belated and puerile attempts to bring the *Omukama* round with a mixture of bombast and trinkets.

By then Baker had fewer than 70 men with him, including the Forty Thieves. He was unable to arrange adequate rations, even for this reduced number, and they lived from hand-to-mouth. The stand-off could not last long. By 7th June, they were out of food completely, and Kabarega now showed himself equal to Baker in deviousness. Apparently making a concession, he allowed a quantity of food into the camp, together with a goodwill gift of seven great earthenware jars of 'cider', the sweet local banana beer. According to Baker, the beverage was poisoned, but to this day the Banyoro deny it, claiming, quite plausibly, that it was a strong brew and that Baker's men simply overindulged. Indeed, it is not easy to think of any poison available to the Banyoro that would have been, both undetectable, and effective. Whatever the reason, the garrisons were stricken with nausea. Florence, resourceful as always, found salt, mustard and tartar emetic and dosed the sick rigorously, restoring them to health in time for the coming battle.

Normally, the Banyoro never fought in darkness, but that night it was noticed that the usually noisy town was silent, although in the small hours there were sounds, as of disturbed roosters and cattle. On 8th July 1872, Baker's birthday, at the magic

Opposite: A young Banyoro mother with her little boy

saa threnashara (zero hour in Swahili time, ie sunrise), a cacophony of savage screeches broke out. Baker answered with the bugle call to action, and the battle of Masindi commenced.

In spite of the tall grass and hutments which enabled their assailants to approach unseen, Baker's disciplined rifle fire, combined with the blue-light rockets, which quickly sent the grass- and reed-town up in a wind-driven conflagration, drove off the attack. A great number of Banyoro were killed. Baker's losses amounted to four dead, including two of his best native officers. He, of course claimed victory: the savages had been driven off, their capital destroyed and their King had fled. But it was to be a hollow victory. The Banyoro remained resolutely hostile in the surrounding countryside, and the invaders were finally denied the possibility for reconciliation and for fresh food supplies.

After burying the dead, Baker lamented: 'My heart was heavy. God knows I had worked with the best intentions for the benefit of the country and this was the lamentable result. My best men were treacherously murdered. We had narrowly escaped a general massacre. We had won the battle and Masindi was swept from the earth. What next?... The disgusting ingratitude and treachery of the Negro surpasses imagination. What is to become of these countries?...all my good-will brings forth evil deeds.'

Baker's words are enlightening. For the first time, we see spelt out the European illusion that was to persist for another century – until the end of the colonial period – and then for a further 50 years under the delusion of western aid programmes. What on earth were his 'best intentions'?...What were the Banyoro meant to be grateful for?...What was their treachery, other than the defence of their homeland?

Facing starvation, the Bakers had no option but to retreat northwards to Foweira on empty stomachs. Once more, Florence emerged as the heroine of the hour. She was quartermaster and she confided to her husband that, anticipating such a contingency, she had for sometime been secreting small portions of millet flour in their metal safari boxes. By now, she had a reserve of some 12 bushels. It would just about keep the party alive, provided they made an immediate start. On 14th June, in drizzling rain, they began the retreat – a column of 65 people and two horses. All their surplus equipment, together with the wildly exploding blue rockets, were consigned to a great conflagration – surely a bonfire of western vanities.

The journey to Foweira took ten days. It was a nightmare. Strung out in single file, along scarcely defined paths, through dark banana plantations and in the dense ten-foot tall rain-drenched grass, where rifles were of little use, they offered an easy target to the Banyoro, who could stalk them at close quarters. Florence marched bravely, her husband's reserve of ammunition in her bosom, and two bottles of brandy in her pack. With a Colt revolver in her belt, she was never more than a pace or two behind Samuel. Day by day, men were killed or wounded, but by 23rd June they were out of the tall grass country and the Banyoro attacks ceased. Next day, they reached the Nile at Foweira, which was safe territory, being under the control of King Kabarega's disaffected relation, Rionga. The retreat had been catastrophic. On the march, ten men had been killed and 11 wounded. But this was as nothing to Baker's loss of his self-proclaimed province and the collapse of the Khedive's aspirations to the Nile sources – not that Baker described it in these terms. In his account, the battle of Masindi was a victory, the retreat a temporary set back, and he was already formulating plans for a reconquest.

They had achieved nothing but immense disruption and loss and they had antagonised Bunyoro permanently. The self-deluded Baker, of course, did not see it in this light. '... The victory was gained, and I could only thank God for the great success that had attended all my efforts. The slave hunting was now at an end throughout an immense district...' He was of course massaging the facts for the benefit of the Khedive and of the British establishment, following the well known principle that, if you are going to tell an untruth, better let it be a big one. But his four-year contract was almost expired and he still had to get his rump column back to Gondokoro, in time to catch the annual flood down to Khartoum. 'Every cloud had passed away,' he wrote, 'and the term of my office expired in peace and sunshine. In this result, I humbly traced God's blessing.' From this magical scene, worthy of a Wagner's opera, the grand illusionist and his golden-haired assistant turned their backs on Africa, to be replaced, in due course, by an even greater dreamer, Colonel Charles Gordon, whose fantasies were to lead to disaster on an even greater scale.

Notwithstanding the chapter of calamities that had marked the four years of his commission, the status of his Lake Albert must always have been at the back of Baker's mind. At Masindi, he made this promise in his diary: 'I shall thoroughly explore the Albert Nyanza in boats and afterwards proceed to King Mutesa of Uganda.' It was to remain a pipe dream. While he frequently speculated on this subject himself, he fervently deprecated speculation in others: 'I do not love to dwell upon geographical theories as I have a strong objection to geographical assertions, unless proved by actual inspection...Thus I shall give to the public the unpolished statements [of naive indigenes] precisely as I have heard them [through fallible interpretation] upon which data [that is to say anecdotage] theoretical geographers may form their own opinion.' Oh dear! Blinded by a serious bout of African madness, step by step, he sinks deeper into the slough. His only actual observation had been on that fateful day of March 1874, when, from the heights above Vacovia and intoxicated in equal measure by success and fever, and the adoration of his beautiful slave girl, he had stared into the southern haze and imagined that he was looking at Africa's greatest inland sea and grand source of the Nile.

Livingstone and Stanley

1871–1872

Samuel Baker was not the only one who was to get his fingers burnt in the Nile controversy. Even the doyen, Dr David Livingstone, stepped into this minefield. Livingstone was the quintessential Scot of humble birth – physician, missionary and humanitarian. He sympathised with Speke over his difficulties with Burton, but, even so, was convinced that he had backed the wrong horse: 'Poor Speke,' he wrote, 'has turned his back on the real sources of the Nile: his river at the Ripon falls was not large enough.' During his first expedition as an exploratory missionary, Livingstone discovered Lake Ngami in present-day Zambia, in 1849. Between the years 1853–56 he crossed the continent, revealing the Zambezi River and discovering the Victoria Falls. In the period of 1858–61, he followed the Shire River and discovered Lake Nyasa in Malawi.

The emphasis of exploration had moved south, and the Royal Geographical Society sent Livingstone back to Africa in 1865 to seek the ultimate sources of the Nile in the region south-west of Lake Tanganyika, thereby implying that they leaned towards *his* theory. His wanderings over the next eight years were largely unproductive. He discovered the swamp lake of Bangweolo, but was unable to assign to it any geographical importance. He reached the northwards flowing Lualaba River, but was unable to demonstrate whether it belonged to the Nile or to the Congo. The anti-Speke tide was now a flood. Dr Georg August Schweinfurth, the scholarly German traveller, followed John Petherick in the western catchments – the regions of the Bahr-el-Ghazal and the Webb River headwaters between 1868–71. In his book, published in 1874, Schweinfurth includes, quite gratuitously, since his travels never impinged on the area, a map of the great lakes in which Lake Victoria is replaced by five widely spaced small lakes. Lake Albert is shown as being as large, if not larger, than all these five put together. Stanley, in the book in which he describes how he found Livingstone, provides a map titled: *A Sketch map of Dr Livingstone's Discoveries: Stanley's hypothesis regarding the connection of the Lualaba with the Nile*. It shows a confused mishmash of speculative lakes and rivers, based on the Lualaba, all directed towards Baker's oversized Lake Albert. Everyone was getting it wrong and Speke was no longer there to answer his detractors.

At the end of the first six years of Livingstone's last journey, with his supply of quinine and other essentials exhausted, he was worn out and sick. In this state he reached Ujiji,

Opposite, top picture: Dr David Livingstone in 1864
Bottom picture: Henry Morton Stanley

on the eastern shore of the Tanganyikan sea, and it was here, on 10th November 1871, that he was so famously presumed upon by Henry Morton Stanley.

Stanley appears on the African scene as a new type of man. He bestrides the continent like a Colossus. He was neither a gentleman like Baker, nor an officer like Burton and Speke, nor a religious humanitarian like Livingstone, Krapf and Rebmann. He was born illegitimate in Wales in 1841 and given the surname of Rowlands. He was rejected by his mother and put into the workhouse, from which he ran away to the southern states of America, working as a cabin boy.

Penniless, he was befriended by a businessman from whom he took the name Stanley. Caught up in the American civil war and taken prisoner by the north, he turned his misfortune to advantage, writing despatches that led to his becoming one of the leading correspondents on the *New York Herald* newspaper. He was the living exemplar of self-improvement. Shame was his spur, and the driving force of his life became self-justification, expressed as an intolerant egocentrism. He coupled courage with a logistical mind, clarity of vision and a baffling tolerance to malaria. In short, he was a formidable machine for breaking open the still unknown regions of the heart of Africa – fully justifying his nickname, *Bula Matari,* he who splits rocks asunder.

By 1871 there was international concern over the lack of news from Dr Livingstone. Stanley's editor, James Gordon Bennett, assigned him to the task of going to Africa and finding Livingstone. Stanley set off, following the slave trail from Bagamoyo in March of that year. His caravan manager was the now famous Bombay, who had accompanied Burton and Speke. He also took with him two randomly acquired European subordinates, both seamen: W L Farquar and John William Shaw. It is characteristic of Stanley that for his first two expeditions, he chose lower-class subordinates as his companions, both of whom were to die on the way to Ujiji. Stanley was not new to African travel, having accompanied the British Abyssinian military expedition of 1869. He knew exactly what he wanted to do, and how to do it. Even so, at Kazeh, he allowed himself to become involved in local warfare between the Arabs and the African warlord, Mirambo. As a result, it took him eight months to reach Ujiji, for ever famous as the meeting point where Stanley stumbled upon a man he presumed was the famous Dr Livingstone.

Having found and interviewed Dr Livingstone and handed over his relief supplies, Stanley's journalistic instinct must have told him to race back to the coast and file his telegrams. This was counting without Livingstone's charisma. It magnetised Stanley. The older man – Livingstone was 58 years old, Stanley 28 – somewhat muted the prickliness of Stanley's nature, and opened his mind to the idea that there might be more to Africa than an opportunity to further his own self-esteem. The father and son chemistry proving sound, they decided to make a trip together to the head of Lake Tanganyika, to try to resolve once and for all Burton's enigma, ie whether or not the lake was a reservoir of the Nile.

Opposite: This map shows the route followed by Stanley during his 1871 and 1874-75 journeys. It includes Ujiji, on the shore of Lake Tanganyika, where the celebrated meeting between Stanley and Livingstone took place.

The journey took 28 days, travelling in a 60 foot long canoe with 16 paddlers. 'Our ship – though nothing more than a cranky canoe hollowed out of the noble mvule tree... Was an African Argo, bound on a nobler enterprise than its famous Grecian prototype. We were bound upon no mercenary errand, after no Golden Fleece, but perhaps to discover a highway for commerce which should bring the ships of the Nile up to Ujiji, Usowa, and far Marungu.' For an entirely self-educated man, Stanley puts the products of our modern schools to shame with his erudition. As to their expectations, they had heard reports that the river did indeed flow out of the lake, thus contradicting the ones heard by Burton and Speke.

For all the brashness many of Stanley's biographers have attributed to him, for anyone who has followed in his footsteps, with his books in hand, his descriptions are percipient and authentic. Through his eyes, and for the first time, the poetry of Africa, with its dreadful polarisations of sweetness and cruelty, is revealed. It was not only in the field of geography that famous people got their fingers burnt at this time. Florence Nightingale's snide *mot* about Stanley's book: 'The worst possible book about the best possible subject,' diminishes her reputation – not his!

The glorious colour changes of the waters of the lake; the densely forested coasts, '...a wealth of boscage of beautiful trees, many of which were in bloom and crowned with glory, exhaling an indescribably sweet fragrance...' Stanley was entranced by this Eden-like landscape and the strength of his narrative still touches the reader today. From the Indian ocean shore to Ujiji, he had seen nothing like it. Nor had he seen anything to compare with the seemingly idyllic circumstances of the native people, with their groves of palms and plantains, their varied lush crops, and the plenitude of delicious fish yielded by the waters of the lake. All this was in symbiosis with the rich wildlife: monkeys, crocodiles, hippos, giant monitors and spectacular flocks of waterfowl.

Stanley is never afraid to switch from the sublime to the mundane. On the same page of his book he informs us that the good Doctor had suffered from intractable diarrhoea while he, anomalously, had to endure 'excessive costiveness'. Although malarial fevers are always given prime place when speaking of the ills of early African travel, I believe many will agree with me that, at least in these days of effective malarial suppressants, it is the to-and-fro battle of the bowels that most preoccupies the traveller.

Proceeding close inshore, up the east side of the lake, from cape to cape and from bay to bay – each surpassing the other in beauty – when they were within 16 km (10 miles) from the northern limits, they crossed to the west side, roughly at the farthest point touched upon by Burton and Speke, and set about a detailed study of the lake head. They found

Opposite: Ferrying passengers in a traditional hollowed-out canoe

a maze of inlets separated by sandspits covered with tall spear grass. The actual delta of the Rusizi River was difficult to identify because of the confusing masses of reeds. They could not see the main channel until they were within 180 m (200 yards) from it and then only by watching the fishing canoes coming out of it. They invited a fisherman to show them the way and soon had a small flotilla preceding them, 'from the sheer curiosity of their owners.' This is a pleasingly familiar African scenario. The stream soon became narrow and shallow, but it had a strong current rushing incontrovertibly *towards* the lake. In this way, they examined each of the three main channels, and settled all doubts: 'The question, was the Rusizi an effluent or an affluent, was answered for ever: one thing is evident to me and I believe to the Doctor,' concluded Stanley, 'Sir Samuel Baker will have to curtail the Albert Nyanza by one, if not two degrees of latitude.'

It is perhaps the greatest irony of African exploration that, when Burton and Speke viewed the mountain cirque at the lake head, and Livingstone and Stanley searched the delta, unknowingly, they were only a few miles from what is now known to be the southernmost source of the Nile. The skyline that they admired was the actual *Crête du Nil* of the Burundians. Everything behind it – mountain streams, great rivers, swamps and lakes – feeds the Kagera river system and then flows into Lake Victoria and the Egyptian Nile. Intuitively, on his map, Speke had indeed designated the whole mountainous region extending through Rwanda, into southernmost Uganda, and including the Virunga (previously called Mfumbiro) Volcanoes as the 'Mountains of the Moon', much to Burton's contempt.

In 1987 I visited the Rusizi delta with my Burundian companion. We followed sandy tracks among spear grass. Now and then, at the river's edge, we saw crocodiles and hippos in the brown swift-flowing water, exactly as described by Stanley. At the lakeshore, there is a sand spit, and the reeds give way to an attractive short grass. The scene was exhilarating: the immense sweep of the grey-green waters of the Tanganyika sea; the blue and purple mountains of Zaire to the west, and the green mountains of Burundi's *Crête du Nil* to the north and east. In the strong on-shore breeze, several dug-out fishing canoes danced on the white-crested waves. Perhaps these were the very canoes that had escorted the two great men, for *mvule* is a long-lived wood and such canoes, even when leaky and patched, remain strictly local and are seldom abandoned. All about us the water birds abounded and the airy ambience and vast skyscape reminded me of the reed beds of our English East Anglian coast. It would be a dull person who was not moved by the thought of the two men – the young and the old – standing at this special spot, sombrely accepting the dismissal of the false Nile and of its false lake.

The following day, I did what would have been unimaginable for the first explorers, I made my way north-eastwards, up the mountain side in a four-wheel-drive vehicle, climbing by a succession of breath-taking hairpin-bends until we breasted the tops at about 2,100 m (7,000 ft). Behind us, the mountain-girt sea disappeared below the grassy crests but, in front, we beheld the green countryside of the ultimate Nile basin, falling away to the east, convoluted like the folds of the human brain.

Livingstone had rejected Stanley's suggestion that he should accompany him back to England. The older man was determined to return westwards and devote his declining years to proving his theory that the southernmost Nile source lay in the region we now call Zambia. However, the supplies that Stanley had brought were insufficient for such an ambitious expedition, so they decided to travel together to Kazeh, from where Stanley would proceed to the coast and send further supplies back to Livingstone.

They reached Kazeh 54 days later, and Stanley soon sped to the coast. There, he met the 'Livingstone Search and Relief expedition', which included Livingstone's son, Oswald. This rescue party was a rather tardy reaction by the Royal Geographical Society to the disappearance of their most celebrated Fellow. Stanley does not conceal his contempt for the undignified way in which the expedition broke up, its members claiming that Stanley's arrival on the scene had taken the wind out of their sails. Stanley was even more disgusted with them, when it became clear that the members' prime reason for giving up was their jealousy of the American outsider, who had had the insolence to pre-empt the Royal Geographical Society. Such was the pettiness of these men and of the age they lived in! This was the first intimation Stanley received of the coldness and snobbery with which his success was to be greeted by a substantial section of the British establishment.

It is sad to observe the warped psychology that tainted so many of the people involved in the Nile quest. It led gentlemen to behave like cads, intelligent men like idiots and it twisted frank and open minds into dark contortions. Alas, the quest was no longer a sober search for the facts concerning the world's greatest outstanding geographical question, but a competition amongst prima donnas for the *victor ludorum* in which hubris, kudos, vanity and nationalism were the driving forces. In his under-rated book entitled: *How I found Livingstone – Travels, Adventures and Discoveries in Central Africa*, published in 1872, Stanley restrains his anger towards his detractors until the end, but then his contempt is scathing and, as an Englishman reading and re-reading Stanley's riposte 120 years later, I still find it a cause for shame. It is impossible to forget Burton's sardonic epithet: 'Madness comes out of Africa.'

Stanley returned to Britain to receive an ambivalent welcome by the various factions of British society and, shortly afterwards, took on an assignment as a war correspondent,

Overleaf An elegant crested crane resting among flowering plants

covering the British Ashanti campaign in West Africa. He was returning from this tour in 1873, when news reached him, that was to change the course of his life and the history of Africa.

It must be remembered that during the decade that followed Speke's fleeting visit in 1862, life in Buganda had continued unaltered. Neither the rulers nor the people had any conception of the whirlwind to come and, for a while, Europe had no incentive for further intrusions into the region. A chain of disparate events sparked the fuse that was to set off the conflagration. The first occurred at the village of a minor chief, called Chitambo, far away to the south, at a place called Ilala, near Lake Bangweolu, where modern Zaire and Zambia meet. The event in question was the death of Dr David Livingstone on 1st of May 1873, following years of fruitless wandering with a handful of African companions. The story of how his sun-dried cadaver was carried to the coast by his two faithful companions, Susi and Chuma, and eventually brought to Britain, is perhaps the most moving in the love-hate history of Anglo-African relations.

The second event took place in London's Westminster Abbey, on 18th April 1874, when Livingstone was laid to rest amongst Scotland's great, with Stanley foremost among the pall bearers. Stanley had been aboard ship at the Cape Verde islands, when he heard the news of his friend's death. He wrote in his diary: 'Dear Livingstone...May I be selected to succeed him in opening up Africa to the shining light of Christianity!' Later he expanded: 'The effect which this news had upon me...was to fire me with a resolution to complete his work...to clear up not only the secrets of the Great River [Lualaba] throughout its course, but also all that remained problematic and incomplete of the discoveries of Burton and Speke.' In other words: the continuing Nile enigma.

Odysseus

1874 – 1875

The death of Dr Livingstone led to a resurgence of national interest in the romantic ideals that had guided him on his lonely *via dolorosa* to Ilala, ie the abolishment of the slave trade and the quest for the Nile sources. While Livingstone was still in the field, concerns over the enigma left unresolved by Speke's untimely death, and Britain's need for primacy in the search for the ultimate Nile springs, could be soothed away in the knowledge that they rested in the capable hands of Dr Livingstone – a man's who had become synonymous with African exploration. Now, suddenly, there was no one. The voices of scholarship and science remained equally silent and the task of re-awakening the interest in these all important causes was left to newspaper editors, whose support was not always altruistic or disinterested

Shortly after Livingstone's funeral, the Editor of the *Daily Telegraph*, Edwin Arnold, joined later by Gordon Bennett of the *New York Herald*, proposed to Stanley that he should undertake a definitive exploration, designed to complete Livingstone's work and to resolve once and for all the outstanding geographic puzzle of central Africa. Stanley was to map Lake Victoria and Lake Albert and determine their status as Nile reservoirs; to map Lake Tanganyika and find its outlet; to follow the Lualaba and discover its destination. Expense was to be no constraint: the expedition would be liberally equipped, including a 40-foot wooden boat, made in five sections by James Messenger, a Thames boatmaker. Stanley had learned from Burton's and Speke's experience and realised the extent to which their inability to travel on Africa's inland waters had hampered their efforts. He named the boat the *Lady Alice,* as a tribute to a pretty 17-year-old American girl with whom he had formed an inconclusive engagement, from which, in his absence, she sensibly disengaged herself. As on his previous journey, he picked working-class men as his subordinates, but this time he chose them with more care. There were two brothers, professional watermen from Kent – Edward and Frank Pocock – and a young city man, Frederick Barker, an employee of the Langham Hotel, where Stanley was staying.

The sources for an account of this heroic, if controversial voyage, are his newspaper despatches, his autobiography (edited posthumously by his wife Dorothy), his expedition diaries and his celebrated two-volume book: *Through the Dark Continent*, published in 1878. The latter is a hyperbolically expanded – but highly readable – version of the diaries. There are notable discrepancies between these various sources and it is not always easy to decide where the truth lies. Explorers who travelled in pairs – Burton and Speke,

Opposite: Mehedehet antelope

Speke and Grant – had their companion's critical eye exercising some sort of quality control over what they wrote. Stanley, his three subordinates having died on the journey, was free to massage the facts to please his readership, cover up his mistakes and promote his reputation. But in this respect, he is certainly no more culpable than Baker.

Stanley and his companions' journey, up the old route from Bagamoyo to Ugogo, was marked by the customary troubles: desertions, thefts, blackmail and fever. Hearing reports of disturbances in the region south of lake Victoria, where the warlord Mirambo was stalking the land with his Rugaruga bandits, he decided to turn to the northwest

Above: Looking out to sea near Bagamoyo. This picture was taken from inside one of the many caves along the coastline.

at Mpwapwa and to pioneer a short cut to the shore of the lake. During this desperate passage, one of the two brothers, Edward Pocock, died of typhoid and the expedition clashed with the Waturu tribe. We have only Stanley's account of this tragic moment. He goes into great detail about his efforts at conciliation, but admits that he was forced to make use of firearms to secure passage. A series of skirmishes took place in which he lost over twenty of his own men and killed over thirty Waturu.

The central Tanzanian bushland is a cruelly harsh country. It is a shadeless region of almost impenetrable thorn scrub, cactus-like euphorbias and baobab trees, with a very low rainfall. The bushes have weirdly swollen half-buried boles, reservoirs against drought, and inescapable 'wait-a-bit' thorns that snare you forwards and backwards, leaving legs and arms slashed and bleeding. The region was all too familiar to us in the veterinary department: it is surprisingly good country for the hardy local humped zebu cattle and we kept up a constant operation against rinderpest. Yet, however trying the days were, we knew that we had our Landrovers and well-organised camps to return to at sunset. We were also well versed in avoiding endemic sickness and the Africans, amongst whom we found ourselves, were welcoming. Even so, a few weeks' working safari would leave us physically and mentally drained. As I read Stanley's account, I feel chilled by the agonies endured by his party. The figures speak for themselves: of the 347 men Stanley left the coast with, more than half failed to reach Lake Victoria. Of these, at least 77 were killed in battle or died of disease and accident, the balance having either deserted or been left with the local people, being too sick to carry on. This is a shocking casualty rate: Burton and Speke had made their journeys with almost no losses. Stanley's comment to himself in his diary was: 'This is terrible, but God's will be done.' God's will or Stanley's?

When his column at last broke out from the thorn bush, crossing the imperceptible watershed into the Nile basin, it marched thankfully into the freedom of the rolling Usukuma short-grass plains, homeland of the peaceable Wasukuma peoples and their bounteous crops and herds. On 27th February 1875, 103 days after setting out, the survivors reached the lake at Kagehi (modern Kayenzi), about 19 km (12 miles) east along the shore from the point where Speke had first seen it. Frank Pocock was in the van and waved his hat: 'I have seen the lake, Sir,' he exclaimed, 'and it is grand!'

In the 1950s my family and I knew this wild coast well. For us it was an exciting location for expeditions and picnics. It is most attractive. The reedy bays alternate with sandy beaches and picturesque rocky bluffs – a wild world of waterfowl life – exemplified by the soaring fish eagles and the awkward black cormorants, stretching out their wings on the guano-coated rocks. As long as the visitor avoids the snail-harbouring rushes, there is pleasant bilharzia-free swimming, and just to be beside the great island-studded sea is exhilarating. Frank Pocock and Fred Barker, however, knew nothing about avoiding

endemic diseases. They were left behind with the main body, while Stanley carried out his circumnavigation, for them the coast became an oppressive place of sickness and death.

Within seven days of their arrival, Stanley had assembled the *Lady Alice* and fitted her out. The local Wasukuma had no tradition of lake travel, while his own men, although hailing from the coast, also disclaimed any expertise. Stanley eventually selected his crew (all of whom were Zanzibaris) according to the Army system of volunteering: 'you, you and you, stand out!' Stanley was a sound judge of African character and chose well, for this crew never failed him. He lacked only a local guide and an interpreter. Luckily, he was able to obtain the services of a native fisherman, Saramba, whom he appointed as guide, and of an Ukerewe islander, Lukanja, as interpreter. These two men quickly became indispensable members of his party. The crew, who remained practically unchanged throughout the whole length of the expedition to the Atlantic coast, was composed as follows: the chief was Wadi Sefani, the coxswain: Uledi, the steersman: Zaidi Mgang; the oarsmen were Shumari, Marzouk, Saywa, Robert Feruzi, Wadi Baraka, Mambu, Murabo, Akida, Matiko, Kirango and Hamoidah; the guide, as mentioned, was Saramba and Lukanja was the interpreter.

These were the heroes who set sail with Stanley on 6th March 1875, a day which would become famous. They were 'men to whose fidelity I was willing to trust myself,' Stanley wrote, 'their names should be written in gold.' The same crew, during a period of three years, made the one-and-a-half circumnavigations of Lake Victoria, the circumnavigation of Lake Tanganyika and the trans-continental descent of the Congo (Zaire) River to the Atlantic ocean. By then, Stanley was evidently a fluent speaker of Swahili, the Zanzibari mother tongue and spreading *lingua franca* of the interior, and

Above: *Sketch of the Lady Alice in sections*
Opposite: *This map shows the circumnavigation of lake Victoria by Stanley and his party, aboard the Lady Alice in 1875.*

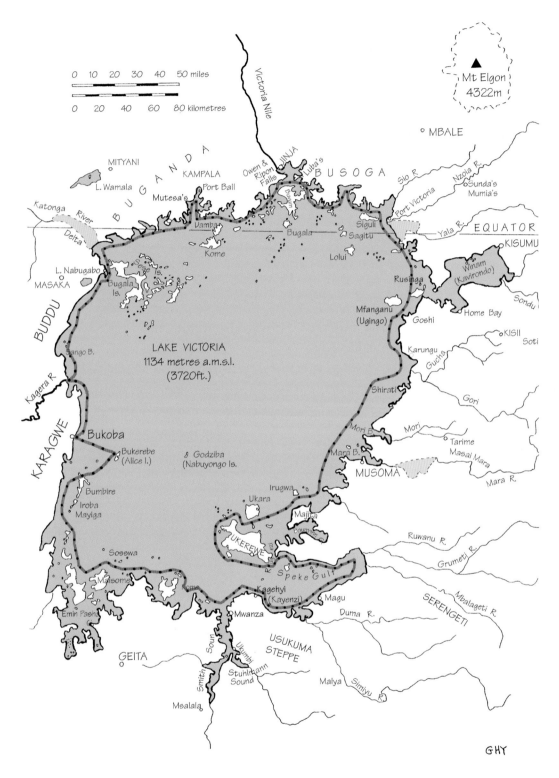

his relationship with his men and their warm response to his leadership, is one of
the most significant and powerful impressions to come out of his narrative. The way
in which an ad hoc collection of individuals grows into a close-knit group, each man's
character emerging, being recognised and made complementary to the whole – the wit,

the wise, the smart alec, the dour, the brave, the ingenious – and the chaff and banter that goes with this – is a joyous feature of African travel and of soldiering. For the European with the empathy to recognize and appreciate this symbiosis and encourage it to flourish, the experience is enriching. The extraordinary thing is that Stanley was able to rise above some of his nineteenth-century prejudices to develop this warm camaraderie, which, allied with his strong leadership, made a success of the enterprise.

Yet these humble men set off with voices of Homeric doom ringing in their ears. The locals assured them that they would meet 'people gifted with tails; enormous fierce dogs of war; cannibals who preferred human flesh above all.' The lake was so large that 'it would take two years to trace its shores, and who at the end of that time would remain alive?' Stanley must have possessed great persuasive powers and charisma to convince them to set off on their odyssey!

As mentioned before, only three Europeans had hitherto set eyes on the lake. The first two were Speke and Grant and the third, whom Stanley scarcely mentions, was an American Civil War veteran like himself, Colonel Charles Chaillé-Long, an emissary of Colonel Charles Gordon, who was at that time Governor of the Khedive's southernmost Equatoria Province, the successor to Samuel Baker. Gordon had sent Chaillé-Long on a reconnaissance to find out what initiative Egypt might take to secure control of the Nile source, following Baker's debacle. Chaillé-Long had spent a month at Mutesa's court in 1874, and actually made a short cruise on the lake, something neither Speke nor Grant ever did. As we know, the two travellers had offered no estimate of the eastern limits of the lake and Chaillé-Long, swayed by Burton's theory, was under the impression that it was a narrow stretch of water that he could cross in a day or two. His African companions were unconvinced and refused to do more than take him on a cruise, for some 32 km (20 miles) to the west of Murchison sound. Thus his attempt brought no fresh knowledge of the geography of the Nyanza. However, on his return journey, Chaillé-Long and his small party descended the Victoria Nile and discovered Lake Kioga, giving us a first and vivid account of this water-lily wetland. He named it Lake Ibrahim, after the Khedive of that time.

Nothing that Chaillé-Long saw and described resolved the question as to whether the enclosed waters of the northern shores were continuous with an immense inland sea, extending down to Speke's Nyanza of the Mwanza shore, 400 km (250 miles) to the south. Stanley, with his boat, the *Lady Alice* and her daring crew, held the best opportunities for monumental discovery. The *Lady Alice* was well designed, a substantial twin-masted boat with a large capacity and a low centre of gravity. It was seaworthy, manoeuvrable and fast, with a well matched suit of sails. The crewmen were new to oars

Opposite A fishing canoe on Lake Victoria

(in contrast with the universal paddles of Africa), but took to them readily. It was natural
for Africans to work in unison, with a fine sense of rhythm. At first they kept time
to their own repetitive songs, the Orpheus of the day singing out the verse, the men
joining in deep bass, on the chorus. This was still the way of my marching askaris during
World War II. Later, King Mutesa gave Stanley's men a traditional Bugandan drum
for this purpose – no Bugandan canoe would set sail without one – to beat tattoo to
the droning chant of the oarsmen.

The prospect was golden and Stanley paints a vivid picture of the exhilaration of their
departure: 'The wind swept us over the fierce waves, the *Lady Alice* bounding forward
like a wild courser. It lashed the waves into spray and hurled them over the devoted crew
and boat. With a mere rag presented to the gale, we drove unresistingly along.' This was
the moment of release for Stanley's powerful spirit: unbound at last, he had before him,
and him alone, a new and unknown world. Hampered by his illegitimate birth,
by maternal rejection and his early experiences in America, he was in danger of giving
way to an egocentrism that would lead him to being denigrated in spite of – or perhaps
because of – his brilliant success in finding Livingstone. The bitter memories, harboured
by Stanley the counter-jumper, Stanley the struggling reporter, evaporated suddenly.
After the desperate events of the march from the coast, the unknown heart of Africa
was at his feet, and Stanley, the explorer, forged ahead, allowing his spirits to soar.

His inventory of place names for the one-month cruise that took him, anti-clockwise, half-way round the lake to Mutesa's capital on the northwest shore, is splendid, but for the most part, the names have proved ephemeral. Of some 50 – capes, bays, islands, estuaries and mountains – that he mentions, I have been able to correlate about ten with the modern survey, while an attempt to emulate his carefully tabulated longitudes and latitudes reveals them to be improbable at times. But this in no way diminishes the glory of his odyssey, nor the acuteness of his written sketches of the varied scenery.

Among other things, he describes the bush-tangled rocks of Mwanza and the boldly rising wooded hills of Magu and Manassa in Sukumaland. Kitaro Island's uninhabited neighbour is a heap of gigantic rocks, enmeshed in a multiplicity of parasitical plants and lianes, while Kiregi Island is populated with crocodiles and giant monitor lizards, living in a strange symbiosis. The Rugezi channel, which separates Ukerewe Island from the mainland, proved impassable for the *Lady Alice*, compelling Stanley to make a complete circuit of the large island (larger than England's Isle of Wight), before rejoining the lake coast to the north.

Majita is a dark mountain, rising 600 to 900 m (2,000 to 3,000 ft) above the lake, while the surrounding plains of Shashi are low and treeless. The coast of Ururi is well populated, but the islets off the coast are uninhabited, with rocky shores and smooth green lawn-like interiors, close-cropped by innumerable, fiercely defensive hippopotamuses.

The Waruri fishermen assured the travellers that it would take them eight years to complete their circumnavigation! At about the first degree south of latitude (the modern boundary between Kenya and Tanzania), Stanley appears to have missed the deep Mara Bay, where the little port of Musoma now lies, and also the important estuary of the Mara River, but he identified Mori Bay, further north, and the lowlands of Shirati and Mghuru He also recognised the Iriemi milk-drinking people, describing them as 'like the Masai.' (The Masai are a pastoral people with whom Stanley never actually came into contact.) Yet, north of the Gori (now Migori) affluent, he heard of 'hills discharging smoke and fire,' 15 days journey to the east, which could only be the Tanzanian Masailand active volcanic region. Further north, the dark headlands of Goshi rise to a sheer 275 m (900 ft) above the lake, a preface to mountains rising 600 to 900 m (2,000 to 3,000 ft), a few miles inland.

As Stanley approaches the north-eastern corner of the lake, his topography runs astray, unsurprisingly, for nature has laid down a conformation of extreme complexity. His large Ugingo Island, 'brooding in lonely solitude' is now known as Mfangano – a marvellously wild island of cliffs and mountains – the ultimate refuge of the sadly mewing fish eagle.

Opposite: Waterlily
Overleaf: Looking at the Ripon Falls from the bank

But he missed the equally large Rusinga Island, the sacred burial ground of the chiefs of the Jaluo people, to the east of Mfangano. It is a near peninsula, and not only did he think apparently that it was a continuation of the mainland, but he allowed it to trick him into missing the finely contorted channel that leads into the great Kavirondo Gulf, which is now called Winam Gulf. The confusion of this huge sheet of water with the quite separate and far distant Lake Baringo was to persist for another decade. Stanley called the waters north of Rusinga Island: Ugowe Bay. However, whoever was really responsible for drawing the map (attributed to Edward Stanford, the well known London cartographer), that accompanies Stanley's autobiography edited by his wife Dorothy and published posthumously in 1914, did rectify the geographical data, but incorrectly showed Stanley circumnavigating Kavirondo Gulf.

Passing through the fantastic basalt arch of Bridge Island, Stanley observed that the mainland on his starboard bow was made up of level plains, and that the lake surface was spattered with innumerable small islands. Nakidimo Creek (Kadimo Bay) was a rough and tumble of hippos, and beyond this they came to the large island of Usuguru (Siguli), after which they entered the 20 km (12 mile-deep) Bay of Manyara (Berkley Bay), a bay that forms the extreme north-eastern corner of Lake Victoria and marks the modern boundary between Kenya and Uganda. The estuary of the Nzoia River, a major affluent of the lake that drains much of the Mount Elgon massif, is on the south of this bay, but failed to be noted by Stanley.

The south to north continuity of Speke's Nyanza had now been demonstrated beyond all doubt: Livingstone, Burton, Baker, Schweinfurth and the others – including McQueen, the loquacious nonentity – had got it wrong, and Speke was proved right, once and for all. It now remained to close Speke's circle by following the northern (Usoga) coast, westwards to the Ripon Falls, the proclaimed definitive source of the Nile, and thence the coast of Buganda to Murchison Bay and Mutesa's capital. This coast is more indented than the eastern one and the lake surface is a continuing archipelago of islands large and small. Stanley describes the pretty views of snug coves and crooked creeks, bounded by low wooded hills and dense plantations of plantain and banana, with a background of grassy summits and extensive pastoral grounds. But the people of Busoga he dismisses as 'arrant rogues, treacherous and untractable.'

The travellers turned their prow westwards and, to avoid the pestering local canoeists, cast anchor well away from land in 23 m (75 ft) of water. Here, as the sun set, they were almost overwhelmed by a typical lake storm: 'The wind...suddenly fell, for in the north-east the aspect of the sky had long been threatening. Clouds surged up in thick masses from that direction and cast a gloom over the wood-clothed slopes and crests of Usuguru Island, which became almost as black as a velvet pall, while the lake grew as quiet as though vitrified into glass. I requested the crew to come aft, and fastening a double rope to the stone anchor, prepared every mug and baler for the rain with which we were now threatened. The wind then fell as though from above, upon our heads with an overpowering force...as if it would bear us down to the bottom of the lake and then...brushed it into millions of tiny ripples. The temperature fell to 62 degrees Fahrenheit, and with this sudden cold down dropped a severe shower of hail stones of great size, which pelted us with great force and made our teeth chatter. After this the rain fell in sheets, while lightning blazed, preceding the most dreadful thunder claps I remember to have heard.'

They had to bail for much of the night to prevent their boat from foundering, but, as morning came, 'the world appeared re-born, for the sky was a bluish crystal, the shores looked as if fresh painted in green, the lake shone like burnished steel, the atmosphere seemed created for health. Glowing with new life, we emerged out of our wild arbour of cane and mangrove to enjoy the glories of gracious heaven...' This little sketch catches perfectly the maddening contrariness of the lovely lake.

Friendly canoeists now provisioned them liberally with bananas, fowls and eggs – but too liberally with banana wine – leading to a remarkable scene in which they found themselves 'dragging about 30 canoes, whose crews were all intoxicated,' and who supplied 'our boat's crew with copious quantities [of wine]...until all were in an uncommonly joyous mood.' Shaking off these hospitable watermen, at last, they approached the large and important inshore island of Buvuma, which almost occludes the noble gulf that leads to the Ripon Falls. Buvuma is an indented amoeba-like mountainous island, peopled by the redoubtable Bavuma and their cattle, who maintained their independence from both Buganda and Busoga by a mastery of the seas and a marked hostility to all new-comers. Repelled with stones slung from rocky bluffs, the *Lady Alice*, while trying to pass through a narrow passage, was ambushed by a fleet of 13 canoes. Rashly, Stanley allowed them to come alongside to parley, when the foremost canoeists displayed their hostility by 'audaciously laying their hands on our oars and arresting the attempts of the boat's crew to row.'

Stanley described his thoughts at this dangerous moment: 'Either we were free men or we were not. If yet free men, with the power to defend our freedom, we must be permitted to continue our voyage on the sea without let or hindrance. I seized my gun, and motioned them again to depart. With a loud scornful cry they caught up their spears and shields and prepared to launch their weapons. To be saved we must act quickly, and I fired over their heads; and as they fell back from our boat I bade my men pull away. Forming a line on each side of us, about 30 yards off, they flung their spears, which the crew avoided by dropping to the bottom of the boat...I seized my repeating rifle

Overleaf: A peaceful glimpse of Lake Victoria with the elegant silhouettes of papyrus plants in the foreground.

and fired in earnest, to right and left.' He hit two men, and then, 'the big rifle, aimed at the water line of two or three of the canoes, perforated them through and through.'

Disengaging from the Bavuma, who 'excel all others, doubly, in savage craft and violent disposition,' they were able to continue up the Napoleon Channel and camp on the Usoga bank near the Ripon Falls. Next day, 29th March, they sailed into a different world. 'From the time the voyager touches Uganda ground', Stanley writes, 'he is as safe and free from care as though he were in the most civilised state in Europe. He and his are in the hands of Mutesa, Emperor of Uganda.'

Kiwa Island was the first Bugandan outpost, and from then on, making short daily cruises to give the King time to prepare to receive them, they were overwhelmed with hospitality and charmed by the scenery. 'From the margin of the lake, lined by waving water cane, up to the highest hill top, all was verdure of varying shades. The light green of the elegant matete [canes] contrasted with the deeper tints of the various species of fig; the satiny-sheeny fronds of the graceful plantains were over-lapped by clouds of the pale foliage of the tamarind; while between and all around, the young grass of the pastured hill-sides spread its emerald carpet. In free, bold and yet graceful outline, the hills shut in the scene, swelling upward in full dome-like contour, here sweeping round to enclose within its hollow a gorgeous plantain grove, there projecting boldly into abrupt, steep headlands, and again receding in a succession of noble terraces into regions as yet unexplored... I imagined myself fallen into an estate which I had inherited by divine right...'

Above: A view of Mutesa's palace. This engraving comes from Speke's published version of his Journal of the Discovery of the Source of the Nile.

The Seeds of Faith

On 3rd April 1875 the *Lady Alice* was approached by six large canoes: at first Stanley and his men feared another piratical ambush, but they soon saw that each canoe carried amidships a number of dignitaries, dressed in flowing white. The senior commander – a young man of no more than 20 – also wore a beadwork headdress with long feathers, a white-haired goat skin and a crimson robe. This young man, Magassa, the admiral of the fleet, was Mutesa's emissary. The boats, riding alongside, he leapt aboard the *Lady Alice*, knelt down before Stanley, and delivered the *Kabaka*'s message of welcome. This included the startling information that, a few nights earlier, the Queen Mother had dreamt that she had seen a white man coming to visit them in a boat. With Magassa's fleet for escort, they proceeded in state, penetrating the broad reaches of Murchison Bay and, on 5th April, they found themselves approaching the head of the inlet where the *Kabaka* had established a lake-side ceremonial camp to welcome his visitor.

From a distance of 3 km (2 miles), Stanley could see the crowds of thousands that thronged the shore. As they approached the land, the people drew back to form a long avenue, and when the visitors stepped ashore, hundreds of muzzle loaders were fired, drums sounded and banners were waved. The first to greet Stanley was the *Katikiro* – the *Kabaka*'s deputy and prime minister – who, with other dignitaries – led him to his grass-thatched quarters. There he treated Stanley to a quick-fire intelligent and polite questioning as a means to establish his credentials. He then overwhelmed the whole party with lavish supplies of food and drink, saying that the *Kabaka* had insisted that the visitors should be refreshed and rested, before they appeared before him. Nonetheless, Mutesa could scarcely wait and, by three o'clock that afternoon, Stanley, with an escort of ten of his men armed with Sniders, was received at the royal pavilion. The *Kabaka*'s welcome was warm and forthcoming, quite different from the caginess Speke had experienced at first, when Mutesa was little more than a boy and not yet secure on his throne.

Stanley describes him as tall – over 1.82 m (6 ft) – clean-faced, with large lustrous eyes (the feature everyone mentions), nervous-looking and thin. His intelligent and agreeable features, his skin which was a dark red-brown and wonderfully smooth, reminded Stanley of the great stone images of Thebes in Egypt. He found him 'undoubtedly a man who possesses great natural talents, but [who] also shows sometimes the waywardness, petulance, and withal the frank, exuberant joyous moods of youth.' Stanley was particularly sympathetic to these – dare one say, typically American – human qualities. Mutesa appeared in no hurry to take Stanley to the *kibuga,* his reed-built capital, that stood on Rubaga hill, a day's journey from the lake. Early in the morning of the third day, he invited him to the shore where, at a signal, a fleet of 40 magnificent canoes sailed

Overleaf: This reconstruction of Mutesa's audience hall now houses his tomb.

into view round a headland, each the pleasing ochreous brown that seemed to be
the favourite colour of Uganda. These canoes, riding splendidly on the grey-green waters,
carried about 30 men each – a water-borne force of some 1,200 strong. Each had
a captain, distinctively dressed in a white cotton shirt, with a head-cloth, worn turban-
fashion. What triremes were to the ancient Greeks, these canoes were to the Bagandans.
In a culture that had no knowledge of the nail or saw, the finely adze-hewn planks were
sewn together with rattan fibre. Each canoe had a high false prow, bearing an antelope's
horns, and a bow-line from which waved silky skeins of grass (designating a peaceful
purpose). These craft had the appearance of fantastic sea monsters. Propelled by broad
spear-shaped paddles (sail was unknown), they represented a vernacular craftsmanship
of surprising sophistication. Stanley's illustrations and his later accounts of the sea war
between the Baganda and the Bavuma islanders, make it clear that the canoes were to be
be numbered in hundreds. They were made in, and mostly based in, the Sese Island
archipelago. It is a cultural tragedy that this highest expression of Ugandan art has been
lost, apparently without regret. Canoes are still made in Sese, but only small craft
for fishing.

On 10th April, Stanley, his party and the lakeside court at Usavara – later referred to as
Munyonyo, close to the spot where Port Bell, Kampala's port, now stands – proceeded
to the *kibuga,* on Rubaga hill. This is one of the several hills on which the modern capital
of Kampala spreads and is the site of the modern Roman Catholic cathedral. Stanley was
enchanted by the countryside of green hills and valleys, clear water streams, pastures,
plantations and woods. After a three-hour march, he saw the hill-top palace, the *lubir*i.
This lofty conical structure of reed and grass was surrounded by numerous other official
buildings and was contained within an immense circular avenue, neatly fenced by water
canes, from which broad avenues radiated on every side, in imperial style. On his arrival
at the centre, Stanley was ushered into handsome accommodation, where he found that
he possessed 'almost everything requisite to render a month's stay very agreeable,' while
on all sides, 'rolled in grand waves a voluptuous land of sunshine and plenty, and early
summer verdure cooled by soft breezes from the great equatorial freshwater sea.'

'There is a singular fascination about this country,' Stanley went on, thereby pre-empting
Winston Churchill's 'pearl of Africa' and the thoughts of many subsequent visitors.
'The land would be loved for its glorious diversified prospects', he continued,
'even though it were a howling wilderness: but it owes a great deal of the power which
it exercises over the imagination, to the consciousness that in it dwells a people peculiarly
fascinating also.'

Unlike Speke's experience, whose conversations with the young Mutesa dealt largely with
issues of power, wealth and western knowledge, always conducted in the presence of
the crowded daily court of notables, Stanley's frequent audiences with Mutesa were soon

much more intimate and restricted to a small group: 'the political burzah and seat of justice had now become an alcove where only the moral and religious laws were discussed.' Stanley, almost at once, determined upon the conversion of Mutesa to Christianity. As Speke noted, Arab traders had already introduced Mutesa to Islam, but not actually converted him. Stanley was encouraged by this. He felt that the King's brush with Islam, by opening the door to the concept of monotheism, would make it easier to move on to the tenets of the Christian faith. One of his boatmen, Robert Feruzi, had been a pupil of the Universities Mission at Zanzibar and, through the medium of Swahili, which Mutesa now spoke well, set about translating the Ten Commandments into Luganda.

At the conclusion of one of these tutorials, Mutesa remarked, much to Stanley's astonishment, that the next day he was expecting the arrival of another white man and begged him to advise on the protocol for his reception. This man, a Belgian, named Edouard Linant de Bellefonds, had entered Buganda from Bunyoro. For all his calamitous failure, Baker's upbeat reports had whetted the Khedive's interest in extending Egyptian influence throughout the length of the Nile. As mentioned earlier, the British Colonel, Charles Gordon (a visionary obsessed with the duty to stamp out the slave trade), had taken on the post of Governor of the Equatorial Province of the Sudan, which had fallen vacant after Baker's departure. He assembled an international corps of officers – footloose adventurers – to further this work and, among these, was the young de Bellefonds. The latter was sent on a mission to Mutesa to try, like Chaillé-Long before him, to determine covertly how best the lake region could be brought within the Khedive's empire. Although de Bellefonds, like Stanley, was a Christian, he was also the emissary of a Muslim Khedive and, without Stanley's presence at this critical juncture, Mutesa would probably have been allowed to continue along the path of Islam, with profound consequences for the history of central Africa.

As it turned out, de Bellefonds and Stanley formed an immediate rapport. The former was a Protestant Calvinist, and the way in which he confirmed Stanley's simplistic account of the Bible and of the Christian religion, impressed Mutesa. The two white men warmed to each other over dinner that evening. This meal must be numbered amongst the more famous of African dinner parties. Stanley was astonished at the Belgian's kitchen, which included such things as Paris brands of potted meats, Bologna sausage, *paté de foie gras* and chocolate. As Alan Moorhead puts it, 'just the sort of things one feels that an intelligent Frenchman [Belgian] ought to have about him in central Africa.' In 1898 Lord Kitchener was to express much the same sentiments, when he met Jean-Baptiste Marchand's supposedly distressed expedition, during the famous incident in which French forces occupied the fort of Fashoda in the Sudan, causing a crisis between Great Britain and France. The French eventually drew back, abandoning well tended vegetable gardens and cellars that included Champagne and other fine wines. Compared with their continental counterparts, British travellers did not march on their stomachs, skimping their way through Africa on the most unappetising native menus and loosing a great deal of weight in the process. Speke swore to the merits of his 'digester' – a mincing machine! Later, Captain Lugard was to remark that the art of African travel could be summed up in two words: 'Worcester sauce!'

Stanley was impatient to complete his circumnavigation and return to his base, at the south of the lake. Mutesa facilitated his departure, on the understanding that Stanley would return with the consignment of gifts he had brought. The King ordered a fleet of 30 large canoes, under the command of the young admiral, Magassa, to escort the *Lady Alice* south. Stanley, having said his *au revoir*, proceeded to the lake-shore with his party, de Bellefonds also came to see him off and, no doubt, to spy out the lake prospects for Gordon as well. Thus, for a brief day or two, Stanley was able to enjoy the uninterrupted company of this sympathetic companion. De Bellefonds promised to wait a few weeks at Mutesa's, in the hope that Stanley would return within that time, but as a contingency measure, the latter completed his despatches, so that the Belgian could take them down the Nile with him, in case Stanley was delayed.

As Stanley took leave of de Bellefonds, we have the latter's description of the departure, similar in tone to Stanley's own account of his setting sail from Kagehyi earlier on. 'I accompany Stanley to his boat; we shake hands and commend each other to the care of God. Stanley takes the helm; the *Lady Alice* swerves like a spirited horse and bounds forward lashing the water of the Nyanza into foam.'

Together with his despatches, Stanley had also entrusted the Belgian with letters addressed to the editors of his two sponsoring newspapers. De Bellefonds did indeed wait, as he had promised, but, as Stanley failed to re-appear after six weeks, he set off back to Gondokoro, surviving an attack by the Banyoro on the way. Having safely delivered the fateful letters to Gordon's headquarters, de Bellefonds was killed tragically a few days later, while on a minor pacifying mission against the Bari tribe.

At this stage, Stanley had completed about three-fifths of his journey round the lake. Admiral Magassa, using the excuse of visiting the Sese islands in order to muster the required fleet of 30 canoes, separated from him straight away, eventually leaving him unescorted. Sailing to the west along the remainder of the north coast, Stanley admired the beautiful views and table-topped mountains that form the restraining edge of the lake saucer. But as the traveller turns south, the coast becomes low and swampy. This is the delta country of the sluggish and ambivalent Katonga River which, as a vast wetland complex, scarcely knows whether to drain eastwards into Lake Victoria or westwards into Lake Edward. South of the estuary, Stanley found the firmer coastline of the province of Buddu (now called Masaka) and passed through the narrow Nabisukiro channel, between the mainland and the Sese archipelago. From this aspect Sese appeared to him to be a single island. In fact, the main island of Kangala is long, narrow and serpentine, and conceals an entrancing archipelago of scores of islands. The Sese islanders provided Mutesa's navy, but they were regarded as backward by the mainlanders, 'the very helots of Buganda' – an unfair dismissal – when one recalls that they were the master-craftsmen of the country's most important art form: the war canoes.

Continuing southwards, the voyagers identified the outfall of the Kagera River, Speke's Alexandra Nile, and ascended it for nearly 5 km (3 miles), until the current became too strong. The lake coast now took on the form of cliffs, beyond which a hinterland of grassy mountains gave a foretaste of Rumanika's pastoral countryside of Karagwe to the west. To the east, there was only an apparently boundless sea.

Rebuffed by suspicious mainlanders at a gravel beach (probably where modern Bukoba lies), they took refuge on the offshore towering rocky island of Musira and here, for a rare anxiety-free day, Stanley allowed his boyish imagination to soar free. 'I strolled alone into the dense and tangled luxuriance of the jungle woods...That impulse to jump, bound, to spring upwards and cling to branches overhead, which is characteristic of a strong green age, I gave free rein to.' He was 34 years old, but in some respects, he was still an ingenuous and impulsive American lad.

Attaining the summit, with its vistas of the lake, its islands and of the pastoral scenes of the mainland, Stanley discovered that it was covered with wild pineapple, ground orchids and flowering aloes. With vivid foresight, he marvelled at this 'gorgeous sunlit world they [the Africans] look upon each day...What a land they possess! and what an inland sea!' He had a glorious vision of what the future could be like: steamers carrying goods from port to port, the industry and energy of the local inhabitants stimulated, the ignominy of the slave trade ended for good and all the countries round about, permeated with the nobler ethics of a higher humanity. Of course, this was Africa, not Arcadia, and, as Stanley descended from the peak, he was suddenly brought back to reality. In a cavernous rocky recess, he found six human bodies in a state of decomposition, one skull at least, split with a hatchet: 'murdered,' he speculated, 'for their cargo of coffee or butter [ghee].'

Nevertheless, a British District Officer in the early 1960s, on his last official tour of duty after a lifetime of service, might well have thought that Stanley's prophesies about the lake had been fulfilled. But who would have hazarded the same thoughts at the end of the twentieth century? Yet the area's potentials are as rich as ever and it will be interesting to see how it fares in the new millennium.

By now Stanley and his men were seriously short of food, and they laid course for a large island, lying far out in the lake, some 40 km (25 miles) to the south-east. He called it,

Alice island. On modern maps, it is called Bukerebe. But the inhabitants would part with nothing more than a few fish and heads of corn, and the starving wanderers were forced back onto a south-westerly bearing, to the inshore Bumbire group of islands, a distance of another 40 km (25 miles).

Famished, they landed at a cove called Kafure on the main Bumbire Island, which is 18 km long by 3 km wide (11 miles by 2), well populated, with rich herds and plantain groves. At the landing place they were met by a hostile multitude that swarmed into the water and dragged their boat for some distance up the beach, confiscating their oars and leaving them high and dry. Tedious negotiations followed, but when all had failed and they were resigned to a massacre, Stanley made a last attempt: amidst the deafening clamour, he quietly ascertained from his men that they had enough strength between them to drag the boat back into the water. Then, posting them on either side, he sent the brave Wadi Safeni forward to face the crowd, with two fine red cloths as a diversion. This caused a check and, at a signal, to the mob's fury, the crew began to run the boat back into the water. At once, the assailants descended on them, Safeni fleeing ahead. As the leader of the islanders raised a spear, Stanley opened fire, his first shot passing through two men. He followed this with duck shot, that landed 'into their midst with terrible effect.' This caused enough of a diversion to enable the whole party to scramble aboard and, seizing the bottom boards as paddles, they moved the boat to a safe distance, only to be attacked by two ferocious hippos, which Stanley despatched, almost incidentally. He estimated that the Bumbirens suffered 14 fatal casualties in this exchange.

The islanders now launched their own canoes in pursuit, but Stanley drove them off. Using an elephant gun that fired 'explosive balls,' he killed five men with four shots and sank two canoes. They were at last able to continue their voyage, with the curses of the islanders ringing in their ears. Three days after leaving Alice Island, his men, having eaten nothing but four plantains between them and drank one cup of coffee each, brewed by chopping up and burning one of the thwarts of the boat, they reached an uninhabited island lying off the southern shore. Here, they were saved from starvation. The island had plentiful supplies of wild bananas and edible berries; Stanley also shot two large ducks. He called the place Refuge Island. They stayed there one day in order to fashion new oars and then, at long last, set course for home.

So it was that on 6th May 1875, 57 days after setting out, the black argonauts returned to the base camp at Kagehyi to receive a heroes' welcome from Frank Pocock and the rest of the stay-at-homes. But there was no salutation from Fred Barker, he had died 12 days earlier, and Pocock led Stanley to the low earth mound that was his grave, on the shore.

Stanley: a Flawed Adventurer

Stanley was now faced with the problem of moving his entire expedition from the south of the lake to the northwestern coast by the shorter western route. This was a pre-requisite, as he wanted to investigate Lake Albert and prove the existence of another lake, further south (Lake Edward), thereby testing Baker's hypothesis of a great Albertine reservoir.

Magassa's fleet having failed him, Stanley had to look to Ukerewe Island to find another source of transport: the islanders made canoes of a similar sewn-plank design to those of the Baganda, although smaller and of inferior quality. Stanley sailed to the island where, following secret negotiations and the handing over of suitable gifts, the young and personable island King, Lukongeh, was persuaded to help. Stanley did not altogether trust him and had great doubts that the King's men would accept to set off on such hazardous journey, so far from home. He concocted a cunning plan whereby 27 canoes and their crews were instructed to sail from Ukerewe Islandto the mainland at Kagehyi, ostensibly to bring Stanley's party to the island. When the canoes beached at Stanley's camp, he distracted the crews who left the canoes unattended, whereupon they were hijacked by Stanley's own men. The dismayed Ukerewe sailors made an ineffectual attempt to reclaim their canoes. Stanley gave them four and they made their way home in these, as best they could.

The 23 remaining canoes were small and capable of carrying only half the expedition and its heavy loads. To compound the problem, they were in poor condition, and many of them had to be re-sewn with cane fibre and caulked with bruised banana stalk, a technique Stanley's people were inexpert with. Nonetheless, at dawn on 20th June 1875, they embarked most of the personnel, and large supplies of cloth, beads, wire and ammunition, as well as some 12,000 pounds of grain. Lacking local sailors, his men had to acquire sea experience as they went along. All went reasonably well at first, but their objective, Kome island, was still not in sight by sunset. As Stanley shepherded his flotilla in darkness, using wax light as a beacon, disaster struck. One after the other, the badly maintained canoes began to founder, the improvised stitching and caulking proving inadequate. It was a desperate situation. In the dark it was difficult to see round dark objects floating on the water – the heads of the crewmen. Stanley hauled as many on board as the *Lady Alice* could carry, even, in his desperation, setting a book on fire to shed light on the scene.

He then instructed those whose canoes were sinking, to hang on to them, the wood having some buoyancy, while the *Lady Alice* made for the nearby Miandereh islets, aided by

Overleaf: *The strange granite formations, known as the Bismark Rocks, at Mwanza on Lake Victoria.*

the light of the rising moon, dumped her passengers and cargo, and raced back to the scene of the calamity. Incredibly, 32 men were rescued from the black waters and not a life was lost. Five valuable canoes had foundered, but Stanley was able to obtain three replacements from Ito Island, and the expedition had to make do with 21 canoes.

Island hopping in short stages, they reached Mayiga on 21st July, the southernmost island of the Bumbire chain, which was uninhabited. Here Stanley established a base, sending most of his canoes back with Pocock, to bring up his second echelon, an operation that took 11 days. Four days before their return, Stanley received a surprise reinforcement in the form of 19 Bugandan canoes, under the command of Chief Sabadu. It was a belated move by Mutesa to make up for the deficiencies of the unreliable Magassa.

The Bumbire Islands form a chain, stretching between 24 to 48 km (15 to 30 miles) south of the modern town of Bukoba. They are separated from the mainland – called Ihangiro then, and Buhaya now – by the less than 16 km-wide (10 miles) Bumbire channel. They were everything tropical isles should be: convoluted outline, rugged coasts and cliffs, mountainous interior of forest and pasture, with plentiful herds and plantain gardens. Altogether, there are about half a dozen islands and islets, but only Bumbire itself and its smaller southern neighbour, Iroba, were inhabited. As we have seen, Stanley had made the uninhabited island of Mayiga his base. This island was the farthest to the south and no more than one and a half kilometer long (one mile) and some few hundred metres (yards) wide.

They were to spend 14 days at Mayiga island, negotiating and trying to secure a promise of safe passage, using the ambivalent Iroba islanders as intermediaries. At last it seemed that an agreement had been reached: Stanley was invited to send a party to Bumbire to obtain food, after which he would be free to move his whole fleet up the channel to the north. To test the islanders' good intentions, he sent a single Baganda crew. On landing, they were invited ashore to cut all the plantains they needed. While they were so engaged, they were attacked and, in the fracas, seven Baganda died, two were wounded, while the rest barely escaped. The whole Bagandan force was incensed, and demanded that Stanley should punish the islanders. Stanley was in a difficult situation. They gave him an ultimatum that if he did not agree to the punitive action, he would never again be allowed into Buganda. At a combined meeting that night, Stanley found his own people solidly in support of the Baganda. He promised to consider the matter and to give his decision in the morning.

Why was it necessary for him and his convoy to pass up the Bumbire channel? Could they not have skirted the islands on the broad waters of the lake to the east? Unfortunately, this was not to be contemplated: the Ukerewe canoes were, at best, suitable for protected waters. Their crewmen were landlubbers, fit only to be shepherded by the *Lady Alice*.

There was no means of keeping in contact at night, when they must either be corralled in sheltered water or beached. Above all, a lake storm could have destroyed the fleet in minutes. The other difficulty was the hostile Chief Antari, who controlled the mainland coast. He was in collusion with the islanders and was daily reinforcing them. It was a case of Scylla and Charybdis.

Even so, if the channel passage was unavoidable, could they not have proceeded in naval convoy style, the slow transports protected by the faster, armed Baganda and the *Lady Alice*? This would have been a recipe for disaster. The fast, expertly handled, unladen Bumbire canoes could, time and again, have cut out individual craft. To lose, even a single canoe in this way, would indeed have marked Stanley as irresponsible. The logic was inexorable. Failing an entente with the Bumbirens, he must either abandon his northern journey and break his promise to Mutesa, or, make a pre-emptive strike.

'Alone with myself,' Stanley wrote, 'I began to discuss seriously the strict line of duty.' Although the expedition's sole purpose was exploration, Stanley recognized that its members still possessed the right of self-defence and were justified to adopt necessary measures for their own protection. He was also anxious to create a good impression for the benefit of those who might follow in his footsteps. The expedition was ready to move towards Uganda, but the waterway had to be opened first. Stanley believed in 'the vital, absolute and imperative necessity of meeting the savages lest they should meet us.'

Accordingly, the next morning, 4th August, a strike force of ten canoes was assembled. It was headed by the *Lady Alice*, with 50 musketeers and 230 spearmen. Stanley waited till noon for a last message from Bumbire. Nothing having materialized, he addressed his men, instructing them that their object was *not* to destroy the islanders and that there was to be no landing. They were to fight the hostile faction from the water, till it gave in.

Arriving off Bumbire at about 2.00 pm, the party found the cliffs manned at every point. Closing the canoes together, they anchored, 90 m (100 yards) from the land, dropping stone anchors from amidships so that the canoes lay broadside to the shoreline. Lukanja, the interpreter, was then ordered to offer peace and friendship, or battle. '*Nangu, nangu, nangu* – No, no, no!' was the reply. '...if you had not come here, we would have come to you.' 'You will be sorry for it afterwards.' The reply to this challenge was: '...come on, we are ready.' Succinct language! But, as always, one must question both the interpretation and the reportage. Since there were no independent witnesses, there is no way of knowing what actually passed between the two parties.

Further parley was deemed useless. Each man was directed to fire into a group of about 50 enemies on the shore. Several islanders were killed or wounded, the remainder scattering into the cane grass or the shallow water. The flotilla then moved close inshore, coming under a rain of arrows and stones. The two sides slugged it out for an hour or more. The islanders had good cover in the dense cane belt, while the marksmanship of Stanley's crew, always questionable, must have been even more inaccurate due to the rocking of the canoes. The Baganda contingent, who up to now had been spectators, clamoured to be allowed to land and complete the work, but Stanley refused resolutely, and as some captains showed signs of ignoring his order, he threatened to shoot the first man who set foot ashore. This restored discipline and he withdrew his strike force to his Mayiga base, assuming that the passage of the channel by his civilian convoy had been made safe.

Stanley and Frank Pocock agreed that the total killed at the time was probably between 30 and 40, with perhaps 100 wounded, of whom many might also have died subsequently. How they could make this assessment is difficult to ascertain, but a confirmatory figure of 34 dead was reported later from Bumbire itself.

The following day, the whole fleet of some 37 canoes carrying 687 people, led by the *Lady Alice*, moved unmolested up the channel. Only about 150 of these were Stanley's own men, the balance being the large Baganda contingent. The canoes also carried donkeys and the bulky goods – Stanley's currency for the next two years of a Trans-African expedition that was still not one quarter completed. Having entered safe Bugandan waters without further obstruction, the expedition could now continue north, along friendly coasts.

The events that took place at Bumbire came to play a disproportionate part in the perception of Stanley by his critics in Britain and America. But the condemnatory accounts lack a proper understanding of the position he found himself in. It is this difficult tactical position, rather than his own ill-advised and bombastic newspaper despatches, that should form the basis for an assessment of his actions. Unfortunately, as a reporter, he was no different from some of the present-day specimen, in not being able to resist shock headlines. Of course, his editors were financing the expedition and he was under an obligation to satisfy their sensation-hungry readers by delivering the goods in the popular style of the day. The result was that the action at Bumbire was likened to a turkey shoot, a personal act of revenge for the islanders' earlier rebuttal, and the near-death by starvation of Stanley's party on their voyage south. There was probably some truth in this, but there was much more to it than that.

Indeed, the historical importance of the Bumbire incident went far beyond the immediate fate of the islanders. If Stanley had taken the alternative course: the withdrawal of his expedition and its redirection towards Lake Tanganyika, the Victoria Nyanza would have remained closed to the western world for an indefinite period, that is, until another Stanley was prepared to take up the challenge of rights of passage. As it was, the western coast route became the future missionaries' preferred highway into the heart of the continent. Within a few years, they were to initiate the process of bringing into being a new country, known as Uganda, whose orientation was Christian and resolutely western. For good or for bad, the course of history was changed for ever.

Stanley's next objective was to persuade Mutesa to provide him with an escort, to enable him to repeat on Lake Albert and Lake Edward, what he had achieved on Lake Victoria. However, when Stanley arrived at Mutesa's capital, Rubaga, he discovered that the King and his full army had left already and were on their way to neighbouring Busoga, to the east of the Nile, determined to subdue the refractory Bavuma islanders. Leaving his boat and people safely laagered in Buganda, Stanley and a small personal escort crossed the Nile at the ferry point, just above the Ripon Falls, and found Mutesa encamped on the lakeshore in elaborate field headquarters, close to the small Bavuma-held offshore island of Ingira. Mutesa had an impressive force of 150,000 fighting men, with 100,000 followers. He also had 230 first-line war canoes and 100 auxiliary vessels. The staunch Bavuma, on the other hand, mustered over 150 well found and expertly handled canoes.

Stanley measured the largest Buganda canoe. It was 22 m-long by 2 m-wide (72 by 7 ft), and 1.30 m deep (4 ft), with 32 thwarts to accommodate 64 paddle men. There were over 100 canoes measuring between 15 to 20 m in length (50 to 70 ft). He reckoned that the Bugandan fleet was carrying probably no less than 8,600 sailors, apart from large numbers of foot soldiers to be put ashore on the enemy island. He concluded that Mutesa could embark a force of 16,000 to 20,000 men.

Since there could be no question of Mutesa providing an escort for Stanley's western journey until the Buvuma war was over, the latter found himself co-opted as an advisor in support of the Baganda, who showed themselves unable to establish sea-superiority for long enough to allow the invasion, even of nearby Ingira Island. Mutesa and Stanley were proved to be equally inept as field commanders, while Stanley, in particular, did his image little good with half-baked schemes, first for building a stone causeway across the shallow intervening water, and then for the construction of fortified rafts. After a six-week stand-off in which the Baganda made no headway, Mutesa settled for a face-saving exchange of gifts and ordered the return to Rubaga.

Two days later, as the concourse of a quarter of a million people were preparing to move, fire broke out simultaneously in several parts of the tinder-dry temporary reed- and grass-camp. Panic exploded and Stanley and his companions barely escaped with their lives. He blamed Mutesa to his face for this horrific happening, although it is difficult to see what the latter would have gained by destroying his own camp and people. Later on, Stanley professed to accept Mutesa's denial, and the matter was left open. Countless people, especially women, children, the old and the sick, died, and it was a downcast rabble that eventually straggled back to the capital.

Stanley gave Mutesa a few days to recoup, before reminding him of his purpose which was to visit the Mwitanzige. This name, synonymous with Baker's Lutanzige, was used at the time to refer to what turned out to be the widely distinct Lake Albert and Lake Edward. Further linguistic confusion was introduced by the early habit of referring to Lake Edward as 'Lake Albert Edward' – an example of Victorian preciosity – in deference to the Prince who was in due course to become King Edward VII. Mutesa responded with surprising promptness to Stanley's request and ordered his Commander, Sambuzi, to escort the expedition with four cohorts of 1,000 men each. The arrangement was flawed from the beginning, and Stanley later admitted that it had been sheer folly. For the first time, his luck failed him and he found himself in the role of an unsuccessful explorer.

The trouble was that the proposed journey could be made only by crossing through Bunyoro. The *Omukama* and his people were hardly likely to accept the presence of a large Bugandan army trampling through their territory. A less pugnacious and more subtle personality than Stanley's might have succeeded, as it might not have been regarded as a threat. But Stanley's basic problem lay in the fact of his support by Mutesa, which automatically set non-Bugandans against him. However, by January 1876 they reached the edge of the inter-lake plateau – the eastern escarpment of the western Rift Valley – and caught sight of a modest sheet of water, some 16 km (10 miles) in diameter, about 5 km (3 miles) away and 460 m (1,500 ft) below them. This was Lake Ruisamba, now known as Lake George, (Stanley's initial name for it was Beatrice Gulf). It is in fact a pedunculated extension of the much larger Lake Edward, but the usual haze denied Stanley the full sighting. By now, the hostility of the local people (at the time this district was part of greater Bunyoro-Kitara, under the authority of Kabarega) and the shillyshallying of Commander Sambuzi, prevented the expedition from descending the escarpment and launching their boat. On the brink of great discoveries, Stanley was thwarted and had to turn back.

We now know that he was on the point of discovering, not only Lake Edward, which is connected to Lake George by a 32 km-long (20 miles) strange lake-like canal, the Kazinga channel, but also, to its north, the Rwenzori mountain range, 113 km (70 miles) in length, glaciated and snow-covered, rising to 5090 m (16,700 ft). Stanley speaks as though he had seen the flanks of this almost permanently cloud-covered range as an isolated mountain, rising to 4,267 to 4,572 m (14 to 15,000 ft). He also reported having heard the local people saying that snow could sometimes be seen on the highest parts. Stanley named this peak: Mount Gordon Bennet (after the Editor of his newspaper!) The name was mercifully not perpetuated, although it took a long time to die. Stanley's Bugandan companions told him that they called the mountain

'Gambaragara', and that in the upper part was 'a hollow surrounded by high walls of rock, which contains a small round lake, from the centre of which rises a lofty columnar rock. It was very cold there and snow frequently fell.' This is a close description of Lake Bujuku, source of the Bujuku River and thence the Mubuku, which at 3,962 m (13,000 ft) are the highest sources of the Nile in the heart of Rwenzori.

The critical survey of Lake Albert – essential to test Samuel Baker's hypothesis – seemed, in the present circumstances, even less likely to be achieved than that of Lake Edward. It appeared as though the whole *raison d'être* for Stanley's return to Buganda, with his great transcontinental caravan, and all the heartache caused by the Bumbire incident, was to come to nothing. He had made a gigantic mistake. But sometimes the Gods relent. Thirteen years later, after an infinity of toil and loss, Stanley was granted the consolation of reaching Lake Albert from the west, being the first European to visit Lake Edward, and to have seen the snowy crests of Africa's Mountains of the Moon. But, for the moment, the combined expedition retreated in muted spirits, by a southerly route through Ankole, and on to Bugandan territory, where the two parties separated: Sambuzi to return to make what excuses he could to his King, Mutesa, and Stanley to visit King Rumanika in Karagwe.

From there Stanley went on to explore the Akagera swamp reaches of the Kagera Nile, to circumnavigate Lake Tanganyika and to complete his spectacular crossing of the continent to the Atlantic Ocean, via the Congo river, revealing Speke's great Nyanza to the world. Stanley played no further part in the fatal European impact on eastern Africa. Rather, in the ensuing years, and as a consequence of his successful elucidation of the Lualaba and Congo (Zaire) river system, he was destined to become the arch-developer of King Leopold's Belgian Congo. In this capacity, he was to preside over a ravishment and genocide of truly biblical magnitude. It left him – and Joseph Conrad – sickened.

Despite the news of Stanley's partial circumnavigation of Lake Victoria and the triumphant vindication of Speke's vision, Burton could not bring himself to concede gracefully. At the famous meeting of the Royal Geographical Society, called in November 1875 to discuss Stanley's despatches, he maintained obtusely that Lake Tanganyika, and its outlet, the Lukuga (recently discovered by Verney Cameron), constituted the ultimate source of the Nile.

Two years later, on 19th October 1877, in a letter addressed to the *Atheneum* magazine and sent from Trieste, where he was the British Consul, Burton who, like Livingstone had never set foot within the central African Nile basin, could not resist another devious claim. 'I need hardly remind you,' he wrote, 'that this great *Wasserscheide* [watery divide]

***Overleaf:** A glorious view over the foothills of Rwenzori*

between the Giant of Egypt and the Giant of Angola [the Congo], which must
provisionally be accepted as the *Caput Nili* [headwaters] was discovered by the expedition
led by me between 1856 and 1859: that we were allowed by fate to see the Nile small –

a gift not granted to the ancients; and that at the time and long afterwards
we were...ignorant of our discovery's worth.' Alas, on that fateful day, with Speke at
the head of the Tanganyika, they had not even seen the 'Nile small'. Whatever his status

as one of the great writers of the Victorian era, Burton could be tedious, bombastic – and downright misleading.

In the same letter, he also tries to imply that 'the very limit of the Nile basin' lay in what is now central Tanzania, in latitude 5 degrees South, that is, by implication, the country first traversed by him. In fact, all this vast territory drains into the inland basin of Lake Eyasi, as the German explorer, Oscar Baumann, showed several years later. Burton goes on to dismiss Stanley as unwise to propose – correctly as it turned out – that the Kagera River was the farthest Nile source. Of Burton, it may be said, that whenever he opened his mouth on the question of the sources of the Nile, he put his foot in it!

It was not before 1881, six years after Stanley had solved the Nile mystery, that we find, concealed in a commentary on the travels of the Portuguese hero and poet, Luis de Camoens, a comment by Burton, included almost as an aside: 'I am compelled formally to abandon a favourite theory that the Tanganyika drained into the Nile basin via the Lutanzige.' Even at that point, he could not bring himself to say: 'Speke was right, I was wrong.' It was not until the very end of his life that Burton came to something approaching an admission. According to Speke's biographer, Alexander Maitland, Burton, then on his death bed, wrote to Grant, saying that every word he had ever uttered against Speke was withdrawn.

Below: Bull elephant on the lake shore

The People of the Lake

One wonders what concept the early European travellers can have had of the people of this region of Africa, prior to their high adventure? They were a disparate group of professional men, clerics and artisans, none of whom had ever visited Africa. Their only information lay in Speke's, Grant's, Chaillé-Long's and Stanley's sparse accounts. Speke had spent a total of five months in Buganda, Grant and Chaillé-Long a shorter period still, and Stanley less than two months, yet it was to the latter that the first missionaries were indebted for the most penetrating, if often naive account of the Hima-bantu culture that permeated the heart of the continent.

While most of the sub-Saharan peoples belong to the negro race, there is a great diversity of languages among them which, nonetheless, fall into two main families: those of a Nilotic type to the north, and those of the Bantu group to the south. One can draw a line across the Nile basin that divides the two. This line is clearly defined by Lake Albert, Lake Kioga and the Victoria Nile, but it becomes more confusing to the east, in the region of Mount Elgon and of the Kavirondo Gulf. It is thought that Bantu speakers have occupied their territories for at least one thousand years and the Nilotic-speaking people longer still. Then, perhaps five hundred years ago, an intrusion by a Hamitic type of pastoral people, slowly extended – either from the Ethiopian highlands or from the Nile Valley – amongst the Bantu peoples who occupied the regions of the great lakes. These Hima people were able to forge a niche for themselves without pushing out the Bantu, because they made quite different demands on the ecological environment. The Bantu were, first and foremost, agriculturalists to whom cattle-keeping was secondary. They congregated, wherever a suitable combination of soil and rainfall could be found. The Hamites, on the other hand, were obsessive cattle pastoralists and sought the open grasslands that provided ample fodder for their animals, but were less suitable for crops. The incomers brought with them a type of cattle, strikingly different from the Bantu's native, short-horned, humped zebu. The new breed, often called Sanga or Ankole, has no noticeable hump (although a thickened neck crest serves similarly as a food store), but they have astonishingly long horns, gracefully curved or lyre-shaped, with immense bosses. However heavy these appear to be, they are in fact hollow and surprisingly light. When the beasts are closely herded, so that their horns knock against one another, they make a pleasingly sonorous, clonking sound. Cattle of this type are to be found today in southern and western Ethiopia, but beasts of a

Overleaf: Mount Elgon – 4,321 m (14,178 ft) – on the border between Uganda and Kenya. Stanley was possibly the first European to see the mountain in 1875. The first European to visit it was J J Thomson in 1883. The Masai call this peak – Oldoinyo Ilgoon *– or breasts-shaped mountain!*

similar type are seen pictured on ancient Egyptian monuments in the lower Nile Valley, so that the exact origin of the Hima herds remains an enigma.

The possession of these noble beasts rested with the Hamitic aristocracy, the *Bahima*, who, wherever they settled, formed royal dynasties and kingdoms. They were the Normans of Africa. But, always accompanying them, were their genetic brothers, the Hamitic commoners, the *Bahuma*, who were the actual herdsmen. There was little practical distinction between the two classes, however, since the absolute purpose of existence for both was the companionship of cattle and the *Hima* and his family were indeed to be envied, since their whole lives were spent in the closest company of their beloved animals, while their staple diet was their milk, often mixed with blood, live-drawn from the jugular vein by a close-shot arrow.

The incomers were characterised by an ineffable sense of their own superiority. To paraphrase Cecil Rhodes's famous mot about Englishmen, to be born a *Hima* was to draw first prize in the lottery of life. Blessed with a graceful stature, often striking good looks, quickness of mind and martial capability, they left the stolid Bantu far behind. These *Hima* overlords seem to have had no difficulty in establishing a superiority which left the Bantu in feudal subjection. This was facilitated by the fact that the Bantus who were essentially arable cultivators, were also consumed with a burning desire for cattle, which formed an integral part of their marriage-dowry system. In a society in which all cattle were deemed the inalienable property of the ruling class, the common mortals could gratify their wish, only by accepting a loan system, whereby they were allowed to husband a small herd, in exchange for mortgaging their family and their lives to the service of their *Hima* lord. In one respect, however, ie in the matter of language – as between the Anglo-saxons and the Normans – the indigenes triumphed over their conquerors. Perhaps because of the regularity, logicality and adaptability of Bantu languages, the incomers unconsciously surrendered their own tongue and adopted whatever local form of Bantu language was spoken in the areas they settled in.

The extent of the Nile basin and of the central African plateau over which this system prevailed, and which, to this day, is still clearly demarcated by the presence of the longhorn cattle, must have been decided upon by the requirements of the breed. Unsuited to the harsh dry-thorn scrub, with its long annual drought, they are to be found in higher-altitude country, which enjoys a more prolonged rainy season. This encompasses the inter-lacustrine plain, the green hills of the ultimate Nile sources and their extension along the east side of Lake Tanganyika, wherever the tsetse fly is not too prevalent. When Europeans first came to this part of Africa, they found a chain of such cattle kingdoms, strung from north to south between the lakes: Bunyoro (according to the local folklore, its inhabitants were descended of light-skinned people, possibly Ethiopian Gallas), Toro, Ankole, Koki, Rwanda, Burundi, Buhaya (Bukoba), and Buha. Karagwe, the *Hima* kingdom of King Rumanika, was an interesting variant: for although the population was sharply divided between agricultural Bantu *Banyambo* and pastoral Hamitic *Bahuma Batusi*, the former group was not subject to the latter, and the two races coexisted in amity, under the rule of the *Hima Bahinda* royal family. In due course, the Europeans were to find that the simplest way to govern such kingdoms was to understand the cattle system and endorse the *Hima* suzerainty, leaving the humble Bantu majority to make the best of it.

But where did the most powerful and advanced kingdom of all, Buganda, fit into this system? Buganda was a remarkable exception, probably due to its exceptionally successful agricultural economy. Their cattle thrived, but the inhabitants of Buganda, whether lords or peasants, also gave much importance to agriculture and were blessed with rich banana plantations and ample fish supplies from the lake. There was thus no reason for the incoming Bahima to subsume the state. Rather, they seem to have been absorbed as a sort of leaven into the dough of the pre-existing Bantu population, creating a society in which cattle ownership, as part of a mixed farming system, was almost universal, but which was not based on a cattle mystique. Buganda had a ruling dynasty, the *kabakas*, who were physically and culturally indistinguishable from the common people.

Bugandan culture was essentially a product of the lake. The latter had created and sustained a crescent of fertile land around its northwestern shores, that had a reliable rainfall, constantly recycled from the lake itself. Thus the people of Buganda were freed from the desperate year-to-year dependence on the fickle monsoon rain system that prevailed in the rest of East Africa. In these regions, every year brings a long sterilising dry season, not to mention periodic cyclical monsoon failures, which hold the people to ransom, repeatedly setting the non-lacustrine tribes back to square one.

Blessed with the rain, that made almost every form of rural economy possible, Buganda had also been blessed, perhaps one or two thousand years ago, by the introduction of the banana from Asia. This was to become the staple subsistence of virtually the whole of the population, permitting as it does, a density of population unequalled by any other crop. Two species of the banana plantain, *Musa sapientum* and *Musa paradisica* provide scores of different varieties, with innumerable uses, both for the fruits and the rest of the plant, that are the basic threads in Bugandan culture.

Stanley gave a picture of the Bugandan peasant, the *mukopi*, as he was at the dawn of European contacts, and which is still recognisable in many respects. 'Decently dressed

Overleaf: Grazing Ankole cattle. These prized herds are found in the higher altitude country, that benefits from a more prolonged rainy season, producing the rich pastures these animals require.

in their bark-cloth robes, he and his wife busy themselves amongst their productive gardens. Little hard trodden paths wind amongst irregular patches of sweet potatoes, yams, peas, beans, tomatoes, squashes and gourds. The plots are bordered with perennial lines of cassava, coffee bushes, tobacco, castor oil and sugar cane. Larger plots yield millet, sesamum and sorghums – needed for beer making. Nearby are sufficient fig trees to provide bark cloth and surrounding all is the deeply shady plantain grove, source of their staple diet. In the offing is communal grazing for their live stock, whether small humped short-horned zebu or red Ankoles with their immense horns, as well as small flocks of goats and fowls – ready meat for ceremonial hospitality.

'Their house is a neat, high, ample-sized beehive cone of thatch and reed, the thatch reaching down to ground level except at the dormered doorway. Inside it is suitably partitioned for sleeping and daytime living, with a central three-stoned fireplace. It is one of a number comprising the homestead, which provide appropriate accommodation for wives, children, parents and other members of the extended family, as well as food stores and livestock pens. There is a love of privacy: already concealed in the plantain grove, the homestead is enclosed by a neat high opaque cane fence. Within this court there is constant activity by young and old: spreading out coffee beans and cassava to dry; pounding and winnowing grain; curing tobacco; sprouting millet to make malt for beer; pressing bananas in a great log trough for cider, the hammering of bark cloth. Even the play of the children – surely some of the best loved and least abused in the world – is based on emulating their elders in these homely tasks. As for the babies, from the day of their birth they are scarcely ever out of body contact with their mother, close swaddled to her breast or back in a sling of bark cloth or cotton, irrespective of her arduous daily labours – an almost marsupial relationship.

'The social world of such a family – who they consorted with, where they found wives, who they helped in collective tasks, who they drank with – was determined by their clan. There were 36 Baganda clans, each a close masonic group with its two totems – usually wild animals, birds, insects or plants with their associated secrets and taboos.'

Stanley's pleasing account should not be dismissed as sentimental fantasy. When I first travelled in Uganda in the early 1940s, such rural homesteads were still the norm, and they provided a delightful contrast to the impoverished and stark state of affairs with which I was familiar in Kenya. Even today, when the thatched houses have given way to banal corrugated iron and brick affairs, the informed eye can still recognise the advantages this lake countryside has over the less fortunate regions of eastern central Africa.

To Victorian eyes this version of the Garden of Eden was flawed. What of the darkness filling the minds of these irreligious helots? asked the churchmen. What of the endemic diseases? asked the doctors. What of their ignorance? asked the teachers. What of their poverty? asked the businessmen. What of their social backwardness? asked the earnest Fabians.

I am afraid, that having been not only an observer, but also an arch participant in western intervention, I am deeply sceptical on these points. For the entire so-called advance engendered by western cultural contact, the loss has outweighed it. Stanley's sharp mind saw that the rural peasant lacked only one thing – protection from his sovereign. Against the arbitrary exercise of power and injustice by the *Kabaka* and his henchmen, he had no redress, although here, in the rural regions remote from the royal court, the oppression must surely have been diluted. When, looking forward to the next century, the royal power was restrained by British administration and authority, while traditional and acceptable laws and customs were left intact, the Ugandan peasant entered a half-century of unprecedented peace, justice and prosperity, but it was at the cost of his culture and tribal dignity.

Having given this sketch of the condition of the Bugandan peasant, as it existed, presumably unaltered, after centuries, Stanley addressed the status of the intermediate layer of the body politic: the lower stratum of the ruling class. This was comprised of the *Bakungu*, or chiefs; *Batongole*, or officers, and between them and the *Kabaka* himself, various special cabinet posts, based either on regional demarcations or duties. These posts were filled by the *Kabaka* in return for services rendered, and the resultant body of notables formed the *Lukiko*, or governing council. While such positions offered desirable rewards in terms of land, cattle, women and slaves, life became increasingly hazardous, the nearer one was to the top, owing to the unpredictable whims of the *Kabaka*. Once embarked on the dangerous ladder of promotion, a man progressively lost his freedom of action. If he faulted, the nod was given to the executioners, but if he pleased his master, further promotion led him to an even more dangerously exposed situation. At the apex, as *Katikiro*, or prime minister, it could be assumed that the incumbent was hated by all.

As for the *Kabaka* himself, as the latest with an unbroken family line, whose oral history when recited, went back some 29 generations, his status was near divine and unquestioned, irrespective of his personal character. Suna, Mutesa's father, had died in 1857, leaving 64 sons who were deemed possible candidates for the throne. Mutesa (originally named Mukabya), was 18 years old at the time and was not seen, either by his father's direction, or his own attributes, as a serious claimant. But, as with the choice of party leaders in western democracies, it seems to have been a case of the *Lukiko* choosing what they thought was a safely manageable character. Mutesa's mother, a minor concubine, had been sold to the coast for a trifling offence, and it was his adoptive mother, Muganzirwaza, who assumed the powerful position of Queen Mother, *Namasole*.

Touchingly, in later years, Mutesa sent a delegation to Zanzibar to try to discover the whereabouts of his real mother – it is not known if this enterprise was successful. Of his 63 rivals, 61 were put to death, only two being considered too young to be dangerous.

Attaining his throne by slaughtering all possible contenders – his brothers, cousins and uncles – and confirming his power with periodic massacres and immolations for superstitious or political reasons, Mutesa knew only the hypocrisy and flattery of his senior subjects and the awesome fear of the proletariat. His sole trustworthy confidant seems to have been the Queen Mother. This sense of isolation may have been a factor in prompting him to exploit Speke and Stanley's friendship, and in his pretence of leaning towards Christianity. Incidentally, whatever the pros and cons to him of adopting this new religion, it had one over-riding advantage over Islam: it did not demand circumcision! Although many African cultures require male – and often female circumcision at puberty – this was not the case among the Baganda, and Mutesa was having none of it. But his fluctuations between Christianity and Islam were entirely political and had nothing to do with religious conviction.

When Speke had reached Mutesa in 1862, the young King had still not been fully invested, and one of new ruler's first acts was to supervise the cutting of the throats of 2,000 people over his father's grave. This procedure, known as *kiwendo*, was a recurring feature of the rites of the country. There was a mysticism of blood. Before the great war drums – some of which may still be seen at Mutesa's tomb at Kasubi in Kampala – could be covered with skins, men's throats had to be cut and bled into them. But strangling was the everyday method of execution. The *masala*, their turbans plaited with the cord with which they carried out their functions, were ever in attendance at court. Alternatives included roasting alive and slow dismemberment. Entrenched in Bugandan history is the story of Mutesa's father's war against his Basoga neighbours. Unable to defeat them in the field, Suna lured them to a peace conference, where 60 of their leaders were seized and bound. Over the ensuing five days, they were chopped into small pieces while alive, starting with feet and hands. The pieces were piled on the grave of his own father. A refined variant of this, was the progressive mutilation of a man, using the razor-sharp blades of spear grass!

As mentioned earlier, Mutesa's early Arab visitors had introduced him to the Koran. Some of his court pages had learnt to read it and had undergone circumcision. But when they refused to eat the King's meat, because it was not *halal*, that is, not lawfully slaughtered under the Islamic code, Mutesa ordered his executioners to seek out every circumcised boy. Seventy were seized and put to death on one occasion, the total probably exceeding two hundred. When we hear later of the Christian martyrs under Mutesa's successor,

Opposite: Mutesa's war drums, kept near his tomb at Kasubi, in Kampala.

Kabaka Mwanga, we should remember that these Muslim children – for they were no more than that – were also martyred for the only religion they knew.

I have already described how Speke walked into this world of arbitrary brutality. Grant endorsed his descriptions: at his first interview with Mutesa, a man and woman were seized for execution, and at another, four women were similarly dragged away. The executioners' huts were close to their camp, and 'night and day the shrieks of the victims were heart-rending.' Grant's book is the blandest of all accounts, but even he is driven to admit that 'Uganda is not the garden of pleasure we have heard it called,' and he describes the common sight of men with their ears cut off, 'not a fragment left' and with amputated fingers. The next glimpse we have of Ugandan life, is the description given by the American Charles Chaillé-Long, in his book, *Central Africa: naked truths about naked people*, published in 1876. Chaillé-Long, Colonel Gordon's first emissary to Mutesa from Khartoum, has already been mentioned. He arrived on horseback among the Baganda, who, never having seen a horse, regarded him as a centaur, until, to their further astonishment, the creature separated into two parts. At Mutesa's court, at his introduction, he noticed a group of executioners lurking near the King. To celebrate the arrival of the stranger, at a nod, the deadly turbans were uncoiled and 'seizing their unresisting victims, to the number of thirty, amid howls and fearful yells, they crowned in blood the signal honour of the white man's visit to Mutesa.' The shocked American goes on to say: 'to protest would have been as useless on my part as impolitic. This was a prerogative that went with the African claim to greatness.'

Chaillé-Long was sickened, and being an uninhibited American in the days before that country had succumbed to the economical truths of political correctness, he was not constrained in what he wrote, in the way the British were by their sense of Victorian niceties. He was scathing of the people: 'as a general rule a lying miserable set', and of the country: 'nothing, but absolutely nothing of that grand magnificent spectacle depicted by the pens of more enthusiastic travellers [he can only have meant Speke and Grant] who would make, to willing readers, a Paradise of Africa which is and must ever be a graveyard to Europeans.' Whether the first missionaries had read Chaillé-Long's account is not clear, but I have found no mention of it.

Stanley in turn, seems to have been blinded by Mutesa's duplicity, commenting naively 'that either Mutesa is a very admirable man...or I am a very impressionable traveller, or Mutesa is so perfect in the art of duplicity and acted so clever a part, that I became his dupe.' The outcome of events suggests that there was a good deal of truth in all three

Opposite: *The forest over the foothills of Mount Elgon harbour many smaller sources of the Nile, among which those of the Sio River and of the Nzoia that drain into the north-eastern corner of Lake Victoria.*

propositions. But whatever his opinion of the King he observes illogically that 'the moral character of the people is far below that of the emperor...they have no respect for human life or human rights. Amongst themselves they recognise only might...this fierce people needs to be governed with the almost unexampled severity of might and power which Suna so cruelly employed. They are crafty, fraudful, deceiving, lying thievish knaves taken as a whole, and seem to be born with an uncontrollable love of gaining wealth by robbery, violence and murder...'

In Stanley's party was an African Christian, Dallington, from the Universities' Mission at Zanzibar. He had helped Stanley commit to paper some elementary Christian texts in Swahili. Now, he started building a church – a simple hut of reed and thatch, but the first church in Uganda – and Stanley, at Mutesa's request, left him behind to continue this work and conduct church services. This lonely black apostle should be recognised as the father of the church in Uganda, before the arrival of the missionaries.

If this was the view of Uganda gained by the first western visitors and the one they projected to Europe, one might ask how it was that in the West, the newly revealed country almost immediately attained a shining reputation as an island of civilisation in the heart of a barbaric continent. The answer lies in the peculiar and circumscribed way contemporary Europeans had of looking at the world. Neatness and good order, cleanliness, politeness, the wearing of clothes, the absence of overt poverty and hunger, were all highly rated social attributes that blinded the onlooker to other realities. Amongst the tribes through which the explorers passed on their journeys to the lake region, such qualities were largely lacking, and indeed, such was the debasement caused by the slave trade, that they tended to be replaced by their very opposites. After months of struggling through drought-stricken, impoverished lands, where the naked people had learnt only to beg, fight or flee, the very neatness of Uganda, its courteous manners, modest dress and ample food beguiled the visitor. That such evidence of apparent civilised culture should blind the Victorians to the entrenched savagery behind the facade, should cause no surprise. After all, it was only what the myopic upper classes of Europe were doing with respect to their own lower-class countrymen, who toiled in the dark satanic mills in their own backyard.

It must be borne in mind that the world the missionaries were about to enter was not characterised solely by the barbarism that we have so far glimpsed, but was also a world with a form of pre-existing religion: animism, superstition, – call it what you will – that occupied the parts of peoples' minds that, in our own culture, are occupied by what we call christianity or, at least, the humanist ethic and the concept of conscience.

The missionaries were to discover that the Baganda had an awareness of a supreme cosmic deity, *Katonda*, which did not appear to deign to involve itself in human affairs, but remained a rather distant god of creation. Of more practical importance were the *lubare* – the gods of providence – the spirits one is dealing with every day and in all aspects of human activities. These spirits were quick to take offence and required constant consultation and propitiation. *Lubare* existed in many features of the natural environment, land, sky and water, notably in the lake itself, and could work in human form as *maandwas* or mediums, beings who would appear as ordinary humans. It was claimed that Mutesa's ancestors had possessed some people, in a process known as *asamide*, when the victim's head is taken over by a particular *lubare*.

Some at least of the missionaries were liberal and broad-minded and did not take an entirely antagonistic attitude to lubarism, recognising it as something elevated above the simple animism that directed the lives of most Bantu peoples. One of the early missionaries, by the name of O'Flaherty, wrote, 'Lubare is not a cold, bare, unmeaning system of devil worship...but rather an attractive service calculated to fill the heart with awe and wonder...a system having its symbols and sacrifices...its priests as well as its doctors of divinity.' Bishop Tucker later pointed to concepts that could even suggest an ancient contact with Christianity, such as the idea of rest on the seventh day and a ceremony, not unlike baptism, when a child is given its name. The idea of *Katonda* riding above all other spirits was, he felt, not inimical to the monotheism of Christianity and Islam. A tenuous contact between the ancient Coptic Christianity of Abyssinia and the Hamitic pastoralists did not seem impossible.

Below: Egrets on the water's edge, Victoria Nile

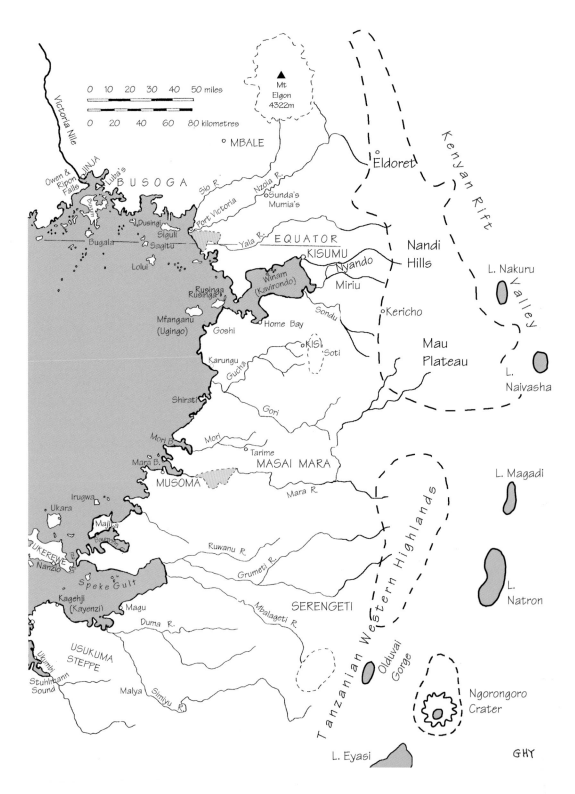

Above: *The country to the east of Lake Victoria, which Joseph Thomson was to travel through in 1884.*

East of the Lake

The exploration of the country to the east of Lake Victoria had long been delayed by the fierce reputation of the Masai people. The Arab slave traders, and the European travellers who followed them, saw the Masai as an implacable obstacle and for this reason had kept their routes to the interior, far to the south. As it turned out, the Masai were to offer almost no obstacle. Although they exercised traditional nomadic grazing rights over vast realms of savannah, that are, to this day, defined by their wonderfully spiritful place names, they were never a territorially acquisitive people. Life for them meant cattle: all the cattle in the world were morally theirs, so 'lifting' them from other tribes and killing their herdsmen, if necessary, was an honourable pursuit which was positively required of them. European travellers, owning no cattle, did not bother them.

In 1884, when the unassuming, unaggressive and cheerfully humorous young Scot, Joseph Thomson, took his first footsteps into the Kenyan Rift Valley highlands, the Masai were astonished and intrigued by his presence and appearance, and nearly drove him out of his mind with their pestering, but they did not physically oppose him. He was able to travel north peaceably, from Kilimanjaro and up the Rift Valley. Leaving the dark mass of the Mau on his left, he made a wide arc via Lake Baringo, broke through the mountain crest of Elgeyo Marakwet to the region where Eldoret now stands and made his way along the valley of the Nzoia to the lakeshore, between the mouths of the Sio and Nzoia rivers. The route through Buganda's eastern window was open and, from now on, European intrusion became focused on this approach. This was to have far-reaching consequences, shattering the ancient tribal worlds and forcing them into the deadly embrace of an alien western culture.

This part of East Africa (that was to become the Crown Colony of Kenya) extended some 643 km (400 miles) from north to south and 194 km (120 miles) from east to west. Geographically, it is one of the most interesting, varied and beautiful regions of the continent. In geological aeons past, it became cut off from the eastern marches, which descend, over a distance of 480 km (300 miles) or more to the Indian Ocean, by the development of the Great Rift Valley. This Kenyan rift, that provides some of the most dramatic landscapes the continent has to offer, cut the ancient highlands in half and reshaped the watersheds. To the east, they drained into the Indian Ocean. Within the valley they became internal drainages, either into the chain of small lakes (some freshwater and delightful, some saline and stark), extending from Lake Natron to Lake Baringo or, further north, into Lake Turkana (Rudolf), that just about reaches into Ethiopia.

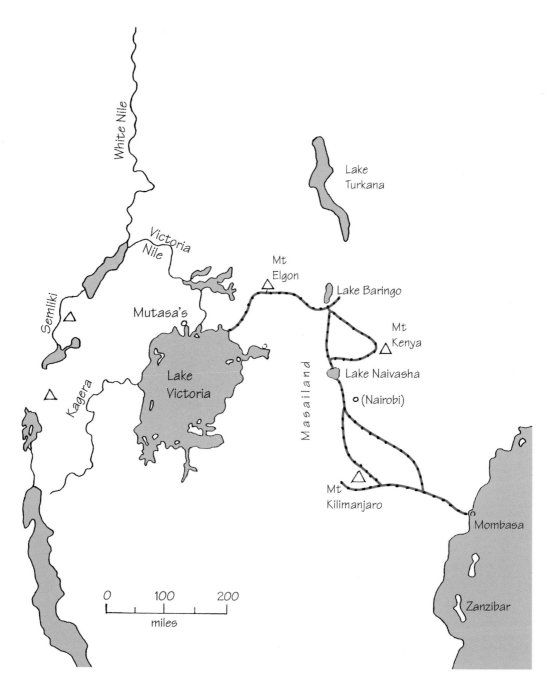

To the west of the valley there remained a chain of highlands, some 400 km (250 miles)
in length – depending on how you chose to measure it – and straddling the Equator.
From their rain-catching north-south crest the waters flow into Lake Victoria, the Nile
and the Mediterranean sea. These high lands have names to conjure with: Karasuk,
Cherengani, Uasin Gishu, Londiani, Molo, Njoro, and then the great Mau plateau
and, on the Tanzanian border, the Loita and Leserin hills. Covered with deciduous
montane forest, that are the product of reliable rainfalls and mists, they give birth
to countless mountain streams that are permanent sources of the Nile.

The ancient volcanic massif of Mount Elgon provides an important addition to this catchment. With a base comparable to that of Mount Kenya or of Mount Kilimanjaro but being, at 4500 m (14,776 ft), lower in height than either of these giants, Mount Elgon is nonetheless a major rain-maker. It sheds water to the north-east to feed the Turkwell River and Lake Turkana; some to the west to supply the Kioga Sudd and the Victoria Nile; but most of it runs south to Lake Victoria's Berkley Bay, via the Sio and the Nzoia rivers. The Sio, in its lower reaches, forms the border with modern Uganda. The more important Nzoia River, not only takes water from Mount Elgon, but also from a great region to the east, comprised of the Elgeyo Marakwet Highlands, the Cherengani Hills and the trans-Nzoia district, that includes the modern towns of Kitale and Eldoret and the northern Nandi Hills.

Further south, the Nyando River drains south Nandi, Londiani and the so-called Mau Summit, while the Kipsonoi River drains the northern half of the higher Mau plateau, which rises to over 3048 m (10,000 ft). The numerous streams of the Central Mau gather together as the Mara River, which makes its way, first south to the Masai plains, where it gives its name to the Masai Mara National Park, known to millions of tourists and television viewers, before crossing into Tanzania to enter Lake Victoria at Mara bay, where the little port of Musoma lies. Altogether, perhaps a dozen permanent rivers flow into the north-east of Lake Victoria on Kenya's shores. Although none of them are very large, their combined contribution to the Nile is significant.

The people in this region include the Nandi, who were later to prove a far more serious obstacle to European advances than the Masai. This redoubtable people's homeland lay in the forested hilly country to the north-east of Kisumu, in highlands above their Luo neighbours' home on the lakeshore plain. Sharing a cattle culture with the Masai, the better rainfall prevalent in their hilly domains, allowed the Nandi to lead a more settled pastoral life.

The name 'Nandi', while universally used, is in fact a nickname bestowed on them by the Swahili traders: *mnandi* is the Swahili word for a cormorant, to whom the coastal fisherfolk attribute a fierce and predatory character. The term is used to cover an assortment of closely related tribes, including the Kipsikis (also called Lumbwa), the Elgeyo, Marakwet, Endo and Kamasia peoples. They are linked by language and custom, sharing a passion for cattle. As hardy hillmen, entranched in their densely forested escarpments, they guarded their independence fiercely against Masai, Swahili and Arab intruders.

Opposite: This map shows the bold route taken through Masailand by Joseph Thomson in 1884 and which opened up the eastern approach to Mutesa's Buganda.

The Nandi formed a primitive society, in the sense that they had no formal chiefs and no concept of villages. They had quickly found out that they must fight the Masai on even terms and had developed an effective military force, comprising of regiments (*pororiet*) of some 500 young warriors, divided for battle into units of about 60 men each. While they had no paramount ruler, they had a profound magico-religious sense, that found expression in their devotion to a senior counsellor, who held no executive powers and was often referred to as their *Laibon* (after the holders of positions of similar status amongst the Masai), but more correctly called the *Orkoiyot*.

While they were famous as spearmen, the Nandi's favourite weapon against a defended position was the bow and arrow. They used heavy arrowheads, expertly made of wrought iron. These they discharged in high trajectory, to fall vertically on the defenders. Such tactics were to be used with devastating effect against the British during the Nandi Wars of 1895–1905. During these operations the British enlisted the aid of the Nandi's traditional enemies. The origin of these wars was the unrest resulting from British attempts to force a railway through the Nandi's traditional homelands.

These Nilo-hamitic people were not, however, the original occupants of the region, for all the while, from behind the high forest veil, other silent uncomprehending eyes

Above: Buffaloes in the open grassland of the Masai Mara

were looking out over the Nile plains. Nandi, Masai and Kikuyu folklore, all trace back their origins to the mysterious Okiek – Kenya's only substantial remaining body of aboriginal hunter-gatherers. Shy and suspicious; gentle and warm-hearted; gifted hunters of the largest, as well as of the smallest wild animals, they formed a non-hierarchical community, held together by a social order based on bee-keeping and the drinking of fermented honey. Prior to the cataclysms of the nineteenth century, they had been widely disseminated, not only in the high-altitude forests of Mount Kenya, Aberdare, Mau and the western highlands, but also on the great savannah game plains. For they lived as symbionts throughout the lands of their more advanced agricultural and pastoral neighbours, even adopting their language, whenever convenient, grafting it on to their own ancient tongue.

Far from being antagonistic, the relationship was patronal: the Okiek supplying their betters with the products of their hunting and gathering – not just meat and honey – but also the necessities for tribal weapons and regalia. They included buffalo hides for shields, hog gut for bowstrings and monkey skins for headwear – as well as forest medicines – in return for the products of farming and animal husbandry. It is not often realised that the famous cattle herding and fighting tribes, such as the Nandi and the Masai, did not themselves hunt the big game among which their cattle grazed, their interest being restricted to the protection of their stock from lions and other predators. The Okiek, although subservient in some areas, were also regarded with a certain awe because of their mysterious lives in the forests. They were sought after as seers and medicine men, especially as circumcisers of both boys and girls.

When the first Swahili and Arab adventurers became aware of these unapproachable people, they asked their Masai guides what they were called. 'El torobo' was the reply, meaning the impoverished ones. To the Masai, people who owned no cattle, were indeed to be pitied. This is how the Okiek came to be known by this name to the invading Europeans. The word was eventually corrupted to 'Dorobo' or Swahiliized as 'Wandorobo' – a name that they themselves still use, rather disarmingly, when speaking to outsiders.

The Okiek were the true ancient guardians of these ultimate eastern sources of the Nile. Their isolated basketwork houses were scattered in the forest glades from which sprang the crystal-clear and sometimes icicle-fringed rivulets of the high catchment. This high, night-frosted world of forested ravines presents some of the most delectable landscapes that Africa has to offer. In spite of their physical isolation, the Okiek would not escape altogether the corrosive effects of western ideas. British forestry officials looked at their presence with suspicion as they were convinced that human presence was inimical to forest conservation. This prejudice took no account of the fact that the forests had been there and pristine when the British first arrived and that the Okiek had lived in them and off them in total harmony for centuries. The attentions of British forestry officers soon changed this state of affair. They were anything but conservationists, and, over the next half century, they presided over the massive clearing of the natural forests, replacing them by sterile soft-wood conifer mono-culture, tea estates and wheatlands.

In 1979, anxiety about the fate of these gentle people, their very existence threatened by so-called progress and the inescapable onslaughts of the modern world, my daughter and I sought out the surviving Okiek communities and made an attempt to bring the impending extinction of this last pre-Bantu forest-conserving culture to world attention. It was a heart-warming experience, but an infinitely sad one too, for we had to leave these innocent people to a terminal decline that will ineluctably mirror the disappearance of their forests – paradise lost. As the twentieth century was coming to an end and as the Okiek gazed out from their mountain fastness over the lake plains, the distant clash of iron – whether of arms or of engines – tolled for them, as surely as it had done for other more dynamic cultures.

Below: A graceful group of giraffes grazing in the Serengeti National Park, Tanzania

The Headwater of the Nile

Earlier on, we saw how Richard Burton tried to 'stretch' the Nile watershed, farther to the south, to central Tanganyika, in a desperate attempt to justify his claim that his 1858 traverse had included the Nile sources. He did not realise that the Mananga, Wembere and Sibiti rivers of central Tanganyika formed a huge internal drainage basin for Lake Eyasi. It was Oscar Baumann, who demonstrated in 1892 that, on this account, the Nile catchment of the south lake region is comparatively limited, and lay nowhere near Burton's route.

The southern lake region was quite densely populated, a reflection of the lake's influence on rainfall and of the fertility of the ancient lake's sedimentary soils. Apart from the large Sukuma tribe, south of the lake, which was fragmented into numerous petty chiefdoms and, therefore, lacked cohesive power, the lake-region people included a disparate collection of small tribes – refractory to change – unpromising material for the missionary as well as for the imperialist drive. This is probably why the region would not attract European commercial and political interests until the last few years of the nineteenth century. The populous Sukuma people and their sparse neighbours, the Zinza, also shared the hinterland. These populations had once been the subjects of *Hima* intrusions, of which only faint indications remained. On the eastern side of the lake there was a balkanised mishmash of small tribes who lived of mixed farming, cattle herding and fishing.

These astonishing extents of grassland and steppe, interlaced with forests, teem on one hand with some of Africa's greatest concentrations of wild animals (for these are the western marches of the much televised Serengeti) and, on the other hand, with the continent's largest herds of cattle. In such regions the traveller encounters land-, sea- and cloudscapes that are awsome in their immensity and he senses illimitable space in the very air he breathes. This is Africa's answer to the prairies of North America and the steppes of central Asia.

As the twentieth century approached, the heart of the continent was still unknown: the complex mountainous region which was under Hima (Tutsi) suzerainty. These territories were demarcated by lakes Victoria, Edward, Kivu and Tanganyika – the area the Germans called, the *Zwischenseengebiet* – the inter-lake district. The inhabitants had such a ferocious reputation, that neither the Arabs nor the Europeans had so far dared to penetrate their domain. This was the last fastness of black Africa, the keeper of the Nile's secret sources. It was destined to witness one of the worst examples of man's inhumanity to man, when, a century or so later, the deep-seated inter-racial hatred of the Hutu and Tutsi populations of the tiny mountain kingdoms of Rwanda and Burundi exploded into a bloodbath. The ensuing carnage was so savage that it left the world sickened. It is from this unfortunate region, however, that the very farthest sources of the Nile spring up.

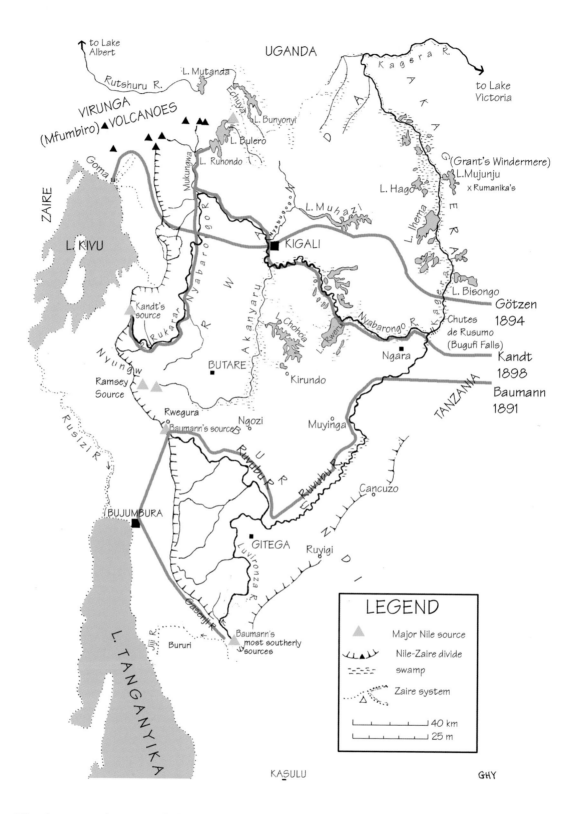

to Lake
Albert

UGANDA

Kagera R.

to Lake
Victoria

L. Mutanda

Rutshuru R.

VIRUNGA
(Mfumbiro) ▲VOLCANOES

Echuya

L. Bunyonyi

ZAIRE

Goma

L. Bulero

L. Ruhondo

Mukungwa

(Grant's Windermere)
L.Mujunju

x Rumanika's

L. Hago

L. Ihema

L. KIVU

Nyabarongo R.

L.Muhazi

KIGALI

Kandt's
source

Rukarara

Nyabarongo R.

Akanyaru R.

L. Chohoa

L.Rweru

Nyabarongo R.

Kagera R.

L. Bisongo

Götzen
1894

Nyungw

BUTARE

Kirundo

Chutes
de Rusumo
(Bugufi Falls)

Ngara

Kandt
1898

Baumann
1891

Ramsey
Source

Rwegura

Ngozi

Muyinga

TANZANIA

Rusizi R.

Baumann's source

Ruvubu R.

Ruvubu R.

Cancuzo

BUJUMBURA

GITEGA

Ruyigi

Luvironza R.

Kagera R.

Jiji R.

Bururi

Gasenji R.

Baumann's
most southerly
sources

L. TANGANYIKA

LEGEND

▲ Major Nile source

Nile-Zaire divide

swamp

Zaire system

40 km

25 m

KASULU

GHY

The three-tiered system of Burundian and Rwandan society had come into being when
incoming Bantu Hutu agriculturalists layered themselves over the aboriginal Batwa
pygmoid hunter-gatherers, only to be over-ruled by the Hamitic Tutsi giants from

the north, (they were indeed unusually tall). This was the state of affair observed by the early European visitors in the late nineteenth century. The Tutsi hierarchy was most entrenched in Rwanda. Here there was a *Mwami*, an absolute monarch, whose royal relations ruled the various provinces. These overlords held the Hutu peasantry in bondage. Since all land was at the disposition of the crown, a Hutu could only enjoy security of tenure by submitting to his lord. As we have seen, the Hutus were obsessed by the universal Bantu desire for cattle, this engendered a cattle agreement system, *ubuhake*, whereby the Hutu would mortgage himself in terms of his labour and military duties, in return for the placement of a few cows. In this way, he was bound up in permanent servitude to his Tutsi master. The sinister symbol of the *Mwami*'s authority was the *kalinga* – the sacred drum – from which hung the genitals of his defeated enemies.

In Burundi the system was similar, but it was less savage, as the *Mwami* did not possess the absolute power of his counterpart in Rwanda, more power resting in the provincial princes, called *ganwa*. In this way Burundi was a conglomeration of federated principalities, with a less entrenched bondage system.

The western world was first made aware of the kingdom of Rwanda by Speke and Grant, when they reached the court of the Hima king, Rumanika, in the Karagwe highlands, in November 1861. Speke records seeing in the distance 'some bold sky-scraping cones situated in the country of Rwanda...a valuable discovery, for I found these hills to be the great turning point of the central Africa watershed...these are the Mfumbiro cones [the Virunga volcanoes], which I believe reach 10,000 feet [3,048 m].' Fifteen years later, in 1876, Stanley visited King Rumanika during his second expedition, also noticed the volcanoes, and it was he who made the first exploration of the complicated eastern borderlands of Rwanda, sailing the *Lady Alice* from Grant's Lake Windermere to the south, up the great Akagera swamp-river system which forms the modern boundary between Rwanda and Tanzania.

Hamed Ibrahim, the godfather of the Arabs in Karagwe, gave Stanley an unpromising account of Rwanda. 'The wanyaruanda are a great people, but they are covetous, malignant, treacherous and utterly untrustworthy. They have never yet allowed an Arab to trade in their country, which proves them to be bad lot.' Of these remarks, one can only say: 'Look who's talking!' All these epithets could be used far more pertinently of the Arabs themselves, whose slaving practices had despoiled every part of Africa

Opposite: This map shows the extent of the Kagera river system with the main tributories that carry all the rainfall to the east of the Nile-Zaire watershed then into Lake Victoria. Lakes Kivu and Tanganyika are shown with broken outlines as they do not form part of the Nile river system. The map also shows the approximate routes taken by later explorers to Rwanda and Burundi.

to which they had gained access. How percipient the Rwandans were in trying to prevent the corroding impact of the outside world. They succeeded longer than most African peoples but, in the end, the onslaught proved irresistible for them too.

In 1879 a party of French Catholic White Fathers entered southern Burundi, but two years later they were massacred to a man on the shore of Lake Tanganyika, at Rumonge, a dreadful confirmation of the country's dark reputation. Twelve years passed, before another European, Dr Oscar Baumann, a German, who was inclined to make his way by shooting first and negotiating later, made the first successful traverse of the region in 1891. He started from Bagamoyo, with an expedition sponsored by the German Anti-slavery Committee, making an original but aggressive transit of Masailand and the Serengeti to southern Lake Victoria, before passing through Sukumaland, rounding the southwest corner of the lake and crossing the Kagera River into Burundi, in September 1892. Following the Ruvubu River, which is the upper Kagera, in 1893, he traced this river to a source, 2° degrees 55' in latitude south, and 29° 48' in longitude east, 1,980 m high (6,500 ft). He gives us a sketch of what he calls the *Missosi ya Mwezi*

Above: *Zebras grazing the steppe country of the Masai Mara, North of Serengeti and on the eastern side of Lake Victoria*

und die Nilquelle – the Mountains of the Moon and the Nile Source – appearing among grassy hills with forested tops. The spot lies close to the present-day small centre of Rwegura and the modern visitor will find that the forests and the tea gardens of the Kibira watershed do indeed harbour delightful sources that feed the Ruvubu River and hence, the Kagera Nile. But as a candidate for the supreme accolade, this branch of the Ruvubu wins neither on the criterion of volume, nor of being farthest south.

Baumann's return route took him via the head of Lake Tanganyika and along the Nile-Congo (Zaire) watershed of southern Burundi, where he crossed the infant Luvironza River (called the Gasenyi on some maps). He proclaimed the waters he found as *die südlichsten Nilzuflüsse* – the southernmost Nile streams. He must have been close to the tiny spring, now marked by a large stone pyramid and claimed, reasonably enough, by the Burundians, as the true, farthest and most southerly source of the Nile.

As Baumann returned to the coast in 1893, another German expedition, under the command of Count von Götzen, was setting out on a transcontinental journey. In May 1894 von Götzen crossed the Kagera, further north than Baumann, downstream of the Ruvubu-Nyabarongo confluence, and hence entered Rwanda rather than Burundi. Marching by the southern shores of the beautiful Lake Muhazi, he passed though the hill-top village of Kigali, headquarters of Musinga, the *Mwami* of Rwanda, where the German Residency would eventually be established and where the modern tiny capital of Rwanda stands. Then, crossing innumerable hills and valleys – Rwanda's lovely *Mille Collines* region – von Götzen arrived at the upper reaches of the Nyabarongo, identifying it correctly as a major source of the Kagera Nile.

In June he reached the so-called 'Mfumbiro' volcanoes, and for the first time, we hear their proper Rwandese name: 'Virunga'. The volcano he called 'Tschannia-Gongo' – now known as Nyiragongo – was in eruption and the expedition noted the red glow in the night sky as they approached. Von Götzen made an ascent and circuit of the caldera, and gives a dramatic picture of the erupting vent. Nyiragongo is 3,474 m high (11,400 ft) and this was the first recorded ascent of one of the amazing cluster of eight giant cones, varying in height from 3,352 to 4,511 m (11,000 to 14,800 ft) which give a sense of moonscape fantasy to this heartland of the continent. Here, at last, he came to Lake Kivu (of which one has a splendid aerial view from the summit of Nyiragongo), the elusive lake, so often mentioned in native reports but which, until then, had not been seen by European eyes. As anyone must be, he was enchanted by the beauty of its turquoise waters. A few years later, Dr Milbraed, botanist to the Duke of Mecklenberg's 1910 expedition, wrote, 'For a combination of comeliness and magnitude, of peaceful bays and deep fjords, of blest islands and skytowering mountains, none can rival Kivu.' This exquisite lake was in aeons past the most remote and, surely, the most beautiful source of the Nile, the headwater of an extended Rutshuru River, affluent of Lake Edward. But the volcanic upheavals of the Virungas which, to this day, still boil the waters of the northwest corner of the lake, ponded and forced it to find a reverse exit, via the Rusizi River, into Lake Tanganyika and from there to the Congo.

The Rusizi flows southwards out of Lake Kivu, down to Lake Tanganyika. It forms part of the Congo (Zaire) system and the river and the two lakes make a credible political boundary between Rwanda-Burundi and the Congo basin. Within Rwanda-Burundi, another explorer, Ramsey, traced the upper Ruvubu River as well as the Akanyaru, and came to the conclusion that the latter, situated in the south Nyungwa mountain forest, offered a more convincing source of the Nile.

The last great German exploratory expedition to Rwanda-Burundi took place at the close of the century and it was led by the most outstanding personality Germany ever sent to the region. Dr Richard Kandt was variously described as a medical doctor, a scientist (certainly a zoologist), a poet and an eccentric, and he was credited with an original mind and a sardonic sense of humour. He was perhaps the nearest the Germans came to a Richard Burton. Like him, Kandt evoked strong and contradictory feelings in some people. René Lemarchand quotes a certain Father A Van Overschelde who obviously did not approve of Richard Kandt: 'a Jew, very intelligent, occasionally dabbling in poetry, short, anaemic looking, olive-complexioned. The bile to which he owed his complexion, did not run only under his skin: he was evil minded...[he did] not act in a straightforward manner. He excelled at tearing things down in the dark, slyly, like a cat.'

Kandt's ostensible objective was the final resolution of the question of the ultimate sources of the Nile. In May 1898 he crossed the Kagera at its confluence with the Ruvubu, where the present Rwanda-Tanzania road bridge spans the river, discovering the spectacular waterfall, now called *les Chûtes de Rusumo*, but which was known earlier as the Bugufi Falls. He followed the Kagera Nile upstream, to the point where it is formed by the union of the Akanyaru River and of the Nyabarongo. He then followed the Nyabarongo River for six days and discovered the delectable waterscape region formed by the Bulero and the Ruhondo lakes, projected against the dramatic backcloth of the Virunga volcanoes, making them, without question, the most attractive source of the Kagera Nile. But in terms of volume of water, Kandt now correctly pursued the Nyabarongo southwards to the point where, as the Rukarara, it rises among the forests of the mountains of northern Nyungwa, on the watershed with Lake Kivu and the Congo system. His Kagera source, in latitude 2° 24' south, longitude 29° 18' east, situated in Rwanda's last remaining great forest,

Opposite: A delightful small waterfalls in Rwanda. This is one of the small sources of the Nile and forms part of the Kagera river system.
Overleaf: The confluence of the Ruvubu and Nyabarongo rivers, forming the Kagera River, at Rusumo.

is certainly a strong contender, and is claimed by the Rwandans, to this day, as their very own *Source du Nil.*

A rare British view of this remote, savage and beautiful region was provided by a young Cambridge undergraduate, E S Grogan, who in the final years of the nineteenth century, made his celebrated walk from Cape Town to Cairo (an early example of the year-off backpacking). Journeying up the Rusisi valley in 1899, he reached Lake Kivu and met Dr Kandt at his scientific base of Bergfrieden, at Ishangi. Even in those early days, Grogan was amazed to see the sophisticated and intensive way in which the African farmers made use of the fertile volcanic soils of the region, with mountain terracing, irrigation and swamp drainage. Alas, he was also struck by the extent of deforestation. The native troops in the neighbouring ill-defined Belgian Congo had mutinied, and Grogan, on his way to the southern end of Lake Edward, had to pass through a veritable Dante's inferno of social unrest, cannibalism and smouldering lava flows, all set amongst some of the loveliest scenery Africa has to offer. A century later, he would have found an even worse inferno. Perceptively, he commented on the 'abject servility' of the Hutu towards the Tutsi – 'a situation of hatred without friction – a far reaching and effectual feudal system.' This *modus vivendi* was not to remain friction-free. It harboured a powder keg. of racial hatred and, during the second half of the twentieth century, it exploded, bringing about a series of successive genocides, that rank among the worst ever witnessed.

Opposite: *The infant Rutshuru River*
Below: *The Virunga volcanoes, or the Mfumbiro mountains, as they used to be known. They harbour some of the highest sources of the Nile.*

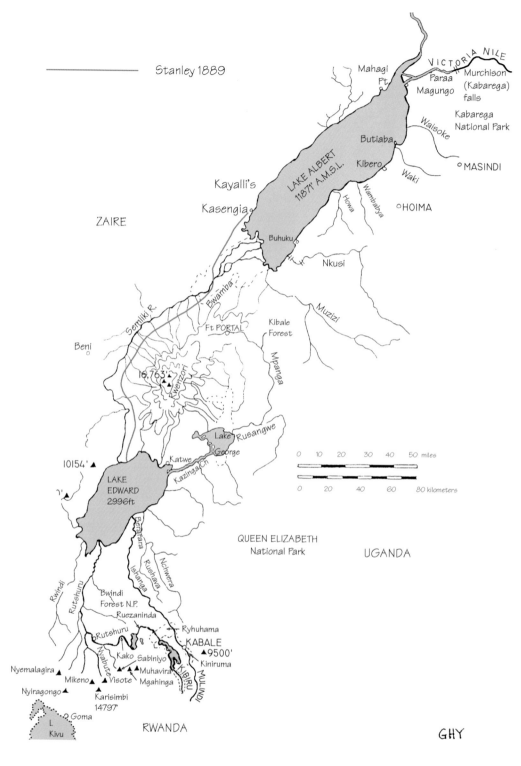

Above: This map shows the Semliki river system taking its catchment from the snows of the Rwenzori Mountains and, further south, from the Virunga Volcano region, via Lake Edward. Also shown is the approximate route south taken by Stanley's expedition in 1889, when he first saw the snows of the Rwenzori mountains.

The Nile Springs

I have told how, in 1861, when Speke was staying with king Rumanika of Karagwe, he had, one evening, glimpsed 'bold sky-scraping volcanic cones,' 80 km (50 miles) to the west, in unknown Rwanda. Overshadowed, though he was by Burton's intellect and overwhelming personality, Speke nonetheless astonishes us with his flair, for he at once concluded that he had 'found these [the volcanoes] to be the great turning point of the central African watershed.' And, of course, that is exactly what they are.

The modern traveller who wishes to see the ultimate Nile and Congo springs, if he will but make the considerable effort involved in climbing these steep and densely vegetated volcanic cones – and should the unpredictable meteoric conditions allow – will find Speke's words confirmed. Standing on one of the highest summits, say Muhabura: 4,127 m (13,540 ft) to the east, or Karisimbi: 4,507 m (14,786 ft) to the west or Sabinyo: 3,674 m (12,053 ft) high (the summit of Sabinyo marks the point where the modern borders of Uganda, Rwanda and the Congo (Zaire) meet. The traveller can observe how the waters shed along the southern flanks of the Virunga barrier, across the western Rift valley, flow towards Lake Kivu and the Congo system, whereas to the east, west and north, they flow down to the Nile. Here, however, the dramatic landscape must be studied carefully, for we are at the sources of not *one* Nile, but of two. They are the progenitors of two great and distinct water systems that, only after many hundreds of miles – comprising the Bantu-hamitic heart of the continent – at last come together in lake Albert, to form the White Nile of the Sudan and Egypt.

The lesser of these two systems is the Semliki Nile, the Nile of the western Rift Valley. Its southerly sources are the mountain torrents of the northern and western flanks of the Virunga volcanoes. They become somewhat sluggish as they reach and cross the ancient exposed plains of Lake Edward, where they become the Rutshuru and other streams. More easterly affluents have their source in the delightful miniature lake district, formed by Lake Bunyoni and Lake Mutanda, with their headwater swamps. Others start in the Bwindi gorilla forests (the so-called Impenetrable Forest), all, at last, reaching Lake Edward across the game savannahs of the southern marches of the Queen Elizabeth National Park, in the form of the Ishanga River. Lake Edward is a basin, linked with Lake George by the Kazinga channel, and it is the latter – Stanley's Beatrice Gulf, a natural fish farm of enormous productivity – that provides Lake Edward with its major inflow, originating from the picturesque Mpanga River. It collects most of the heavy rainfall of the eastern flanks of the Rwenzori range, as well as that of the Kibale forest region of western Uganda, which is notable for its chimpanzee and other primate populations.

Most of the southern watershed of the Rwenzori flows directly into Lake Edward by means of the Namagasani and other rivers, starting their lives as delectable crystal-clear icy mountain torrents and tarns, to end up crossing the arid plains of the old lake bed.

It is these affluents, together with the short run-off from the western Rift escarpment, that sustain the weirdly hazed lake. All this water leaves it by the north-western outlet, where the Semliki starts its life as a strong stream some 28 m wide (30 yards). This dynamic river of sunken gorges, roaring cataracts and secret forest tunnels, was followed upstream by Stanley, from Lake Albert, during his 1889 withdrawal to the east coast with Emin Pasha and his Egyptian refugees.* Earlier in that year two of Stanley's officers, Parke and Jephson, had made the first sighting by Europeans of the snow-capped Rwenzori massif which rises to 5,090 m (16,700 ft). This sighting was shortly confirmed by Stanley himself, who declared that the summits glimpsed from the ancient Greeks were one and the same. As his column made its painfully slow passage of the steep western flanks of the mountains, between the foothills and the river, Stanley recorded some 60 substantial torrents, all adding their water to the Semliki. In due course, he realised that the entire catchment of these constantly snow- and rain-drenched equatorial Alps, with their enclosed fairyland of miniature tarns, was destined for the Semliki Nile, directly or through Lake Edward or Lake George.

As it approaches the southern end of Lake Albert, the Semliki becomes a broad, slowly meandering plains river, leading into a complex wasteland delta of reeds, infested by mosquitoes. It then reaches the great expanse of the mountain-walled rift lake (Kabarega's Lutanzige or Baker's Lake Albert), thus completing the Semliki Nile's catchment.

I have described the actuality of what Samuel Baker had imagined to be the major Nile

---

* Emin Pasha, originally Eduard Schnitzer (1840-92), was a German Jewish doctor and explorer who went to Albania and practised medicine there. He adopted the Muslim faith and became known as Emin Effendi. Around 1876 he found himself in the service of Egypt, becoming a bey and a pasha. Gordon appointed him chief medical officer of the Equatoria Province, employed him in diplomacy and administration and made him Governor of the province in 1878, a post he held until 1889, when he found himself forced to retreat, as he became caught in the Mahdist revolt. Emin was a remarkable linguist and he made an enormous contribution to European knowledge of African languages, as well as to anthropology, zoology, botany and meteorology. Following Gordon's debacle at Khartoum, pressure from public opinion in Britain, prompted the government to send Stanley in 1889 on an expedition to rescue Emin Pasha. They covered thousands of miles with men women and children refugees, ending up in Zanzibar. Emin Pasha soon returned to continue his work and extend the German sphere of influence around Lake Victoria. He never regained his old power, however, and was marching towards the west coast, when he was murdered by Arabs in the Manyema country. *(Editor's note)*

Opposite: *A silver back gorilla photographed near the late Dian Fossey's mountain gorilla study centre of Karisoke, in Rwanda*

headwater. In fact, it turned out to be the lesser of the two great systems, but this in no way detracts from its stunning succession of landscapes which, rarely seen by westerners, display the full dramatic diversity of Africa.

The major headwater, however, is the Kagera Nile, a much more complicated and extensive basin than the Semliki, itself divided into two systems, as was demonstrated during the journeys made by Oscar Baumann and Richard Kandt – one for Burundi and one for Rwanda (see map on page 162). The more southerly system, that of Burundi, is the Ruvubu, whose high source in the forested Kibira mountain chain was Baumann's choice. But in fact, the spring of the Luvironza, a tributary from the south that joins the Ruvubu near the town of Gitega, at nearly 4° south on the crest, above the head of Lake Tanganyika, is unquestionably the most southerly source of the Nile. The Burundians have staked their claim with a monument and a bronze plaque, the work of Waldecker.

The Luvironza – a delightful highland burn – soon grows in size and captures all the waters north of the crests. This is a green and grassy countryside, forming a succession of fold-like hills and valleys, dotted with the long-horned herds and homesteads of the tall and graceful Batutsi cattlemen. The skyscapes are uplifting. The climate is a lovely continuum of spring and summer, and a hundred streams pour their limpid waters to the north-west to form the great papyrus-filled valley of the Ruvubu River, the earth-red waters of which flow towards the confluence with its great congener from Rwanda, the Nyabarongo.

The Nyabarongo collects all the watershed to the east from the north-south crests, which, on their reverse side, feed Lake Kivu and the Congo system. To the north, with heart-rendering artistry, the twin lakes of Bulero and Ruhondo cascade their waters into the Mukungwa River, which soon empties into the Nyabarongo. This splendid river, rising on the Congo crest in the Nyungwa forest, gave Richard Kandt his first candidate for the Nile headwater.

The enhanced Nyabarongo now turns to the east, through the heart of Rwanda's *Mille Collines* region, passing close by the little hill-town capital of Kigali, and, accepting the great Akanyaru river, which originates in the south in the Nyungwa forests, the Nyabarongo then spills into an immense wetland area that extends for many miles on either side of the Rwanda-Burundi border. Tales of this thrilling mix of lakes, swamps and channels had deluded Stanley in 1875. He assumed that it was a single stretch of water and took it for yet another great lake, naming it Lake Alexandra. In fact, the greatest extent of open water, Lake Rweru – one of many – is only about 16 by 8 km in extent (10 by 5 miles), although the total extent of this Akanyaru wetland region is perhaps 65 km by 33 (40 miles by 20). Freeing itself from this complex, the Nyabarongo then flows straight and true between its papyrus banks to meet Burundi's

Ruvubu, on the Tanzania border, and to form the Kagera River, which, at once, plunges magnificently into a deep rocky gorge – *les Chutes de Rusumo* – as the falls are referred to on Belgian maps.

The Kagera now flows powerfully to the north and, within a few miles, it starts to transpose into an increasingly broad papyrus wilderness, the precursor of the next great wetland, the Akagera. This mysterious necklace of grey-green lakes, brown-water channels and complex papyrus and rush marshes, home of the hippopotamus, crocodile and sitatunga, is the second great reservoir of the Kagera system, some 96 km in length and 32 km in width (50 by 20 miles), bestraddling the Rwanda and Tanzania (Karagwe) border. Only when it approaches the Equator, does it form into a single strong stream. Turning sharply to the east, after a further 160 km (100 miles), it empties itself into Lake Victoria, close to the international border between Uganda and Tanzania.

At the height of the development of the steamer services on Lake Victoria, in the first half of the twentieth century, the Kagera river was navigated regularly by tugs and lighters for 128 km (80 miles) from its delta. But when one looks at the whole intricate network of rivers and lakes that cover the countries of Rwanda and Burundi – an area equal to that of Belgium and Holland, with rivers surpassing in magnitude anything we have in the British Isles – one is struck by the fact that, almost without exception, there are no watercraft, other than the occasional traditional dugout canoes, which function primarily as ferries for foot and bicycle passengers, in a region where road bridges are few.

The Germans had intended to build a railway from Tabora to the Kagera, with a river steamer service beyond that, but the Belgian occupation of the territory put the concept on hold. Subsequently, Africa's love affair with road transport, even in this hilly country, meant that the plans were never revived. The rivers, lakes and wetlands of Rwanda and Burundi thus remain, to this day, *almost* totally primaeval reserves and the stronghold of the minority pygmoid Batwa aborigines. I use the word 'almost' advisedly. In spite of endemic genocide and the apocalyptic spread of AIDS, the pressure exercised by the great increase in population and the consequent need for cultivated land, means that the practice of draining the papyrus-swamp, thereby destroying the invaluable filtration and water conservation functions of these ecological sponges, has become widespread. There is no escaping the fact that, as the traveller emerges onto Lake Victoria from the Kagera delta, just north of the port of Bukoba, sail wherever he will – north, east or south, on the wide waters of the inland sea – he will now find himself in a world of immense and rapid ecological change.

As in Britain the Victorians gave way to the Edwardians and the new century, the railway

Overleaf: The tranquil expanse of Lake Bulero, a high source of the Nile

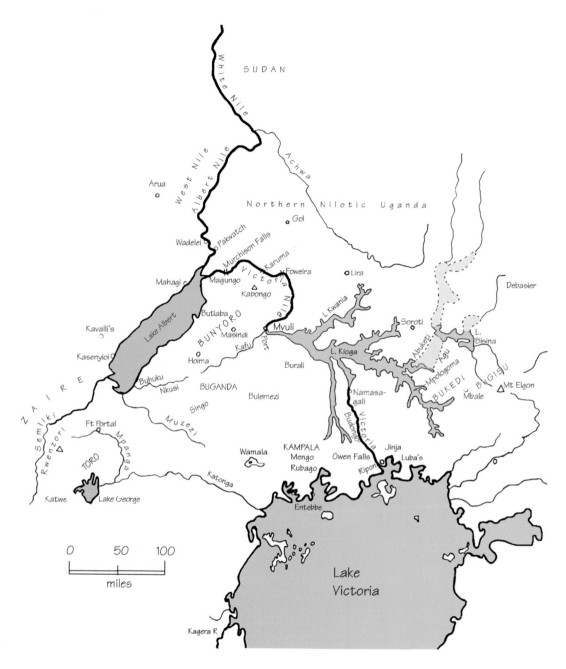

had brought a fine fleet of modern steamers, carrying passengers and freight. Stanley's vision on Mabira island of a Lake Victoria, teeming with tourist steamers, had been fully implemented. The development of transport and travel brought about a dynamic union between the new countries of Tanganyika, Uganda and Kenya and provided the British with a means of travel during the years of *pax britannica*. But, in spite of the river traffic,

Above: This map shows the Victoria Nile system, flowing northwards from Lake Victoria, via Lake Kioga. It flows into Lake Albert, via the spectacular Murchison Falls, where it joins the waters of the Semliki Nile to form the Albert Nile and, ultimately, the White Nile.

the lake waters still retained their well known clarity and an abundance of fish.

In the years following national independence at the beginning of the 1960s, however, a tragic anomaly has cast a blight over the Nyanza. As a consequence of parochial dispute between the three states, the lake services have collapsed almost to the point of disappearance. The waters have now become dangerously polluted, spreading environmental degradation throughout the catchment. This is essentially a result of human and livestock population escalation. That state most feared by freshwater biologists, eutrophication, ie deoxygenation resulting from microbiological imbalance, is now well advanced: Lake Victoria is dying.

Compounded with this, the microecology of the lake has been further damaged by two extraneous factors. One of these was the introduction, in the years prior to independence, of a giant predatory fish, the Nile perch. At the same time, the only species that might have controlled it – the crocodile – was undergoing an equally deliberate eradication. This led to an escalation of the Nile perch population and the resulting collapse of the lake's once almost infinitely varied fish population, notably the many hundreds of species of beautifully coloured and highly nutritious haplochromids, that formed an indispensable protein source for lakeshore and island dwellers.

The other factor was the accidental and inexplicable introduction of the water hyacinth. This species forms massive impenetrable floating mats that suffocate the fish breeding grounds and block the movement of boats and canoes. Modern sailors on Lake Victoria, a century and a quarter after Stanley's odyssey, find themselves in a lost paradise, an ecological disaster equal to any of the better publicised ones, elsewhere in the world.

Lake Victoria is exactly what Speke intuitively recognised it to be: a giant pond of non-rift origin. Its northern rim is created by the 320 km-long (200-miles) east-west reef which blocks the contributory rivers from the east and the west, and the rain run-off from the south. It is a saucer, never more than 76 m deep (250 ft) , but it is even larger than it looks, because the extensive Katonga papyrus wetlands system in the north-west must be considered part of the lake from a hydrological point of view. The northern retaining lip of the saucer is breached only at Mutesa's Eijinja – The Stones – Speke's Ripon Falls, which, as late as the 1940s, when I first visited the spot, could reasonably claim to be one of the most enchanting places in Africa.

Now all that has changed. As early as the year 1904, when Sir William Garstin, the father of upper Nile hydrology, visited the spot, he at once recognised the combined benefits of creating a controlled head reservoir for Egypt's Nile and a regional source of electric

Overleaf: The Kagera River downstream from the Bugufi Falls (les Chutes de Rusumo)

– 181 –

power. In 1907, Winston Churchill, the peripatetic Colonial Secretary, had the same idea and remarked, while viewing the tumultuous scene: 'what fun to make the immemorial Nile begin its journey by diving through a turbine!' During the post-second World War surge for grandiose development projects, a dam was built at the Owen Falls, a few kilometres (two or three miles) downstream from the Ripon Falls, thereby raising the level of the water sufficiently to drown the latter. In this way, this powerfully emotive spot, where Speke dreamed of a wife, has been emasculated. Even so, when the setting sun transmutes it into a river of gold, the scene is ineffable.

At the dam itself, which also serves as a main-road bridge, supplementing the steel rail bridge upstream, the new-born Victoria Nile used to operate ten colossal turbines that, when fully operational, (a state that has hardly existed following Idi Amin's seizure of power in 1969) produced electricity for Uganda and the adjacent parts of Kenya. The excess waters burst through six giant square sluices at the centre of the foot of the dam, soaring as a white parabola, before rejoining the river and surging to the north.

The next 80 km (50 miles) of the river consist of thrillingly picturesque, if almost inaccessible series of wild white-water cataracts, but at the Bujagali Falls one has a fine viewpoint. Speke's Burondogani, where he first saw the Nile, is unidentifiable, but now the river slowly starts to change to the placid stream on which he and Chaillé-Long attempted to make a canoe passage to Bunyoro, via Lake Kioga. In the 1940s there was a steamer-rail interchange situated on the east bank, at Namasagali. (It is now a ghost town, but a Catholic mission school survives.) Here, one boarded the stern-wheel steamer, *Stanley*, for the journey, down an increasingly lake-like, mile-wide river and then across the almost horizonless western wetlands and waterlily reaches of Lake Kioga, before the Nile once more found its form as a river and the steamer reached the jetty at Masindi Port. Here the Kafu River enters the Nile at the spot where Speke and Grant found Kamrasi's capital village, and where Gordon and Emin Pasha held Egypt's southern-most station: Mruli. Downstream from here, the Nile is navigable (but unused) for another 96 km (60 miles) before making a right-angle turn to the west, soon to reach Speke's and Baker's crossing point, known at one time as Foweira. From here the river starts a process of unbridled acceleration that makes the next 80 km (50 miles) one of Africa's most remarkable geographical phenomena. With the increasing power and urgency engendered by the throttling effect of the narrowing rocky gorge, the Nile thunders down a succession of cascades, known collectively as the Karuma Falls, that are at one point spanned by the not very confidence-inspiring Bailey Bridge, which is one of Uganda's few access routes to its immense northern territories.

This final westward race of the Victoria Nile is largely inaccessible to man: it is the primaeval northern border of the Kabarega (once Murchison) National Park, and it reaches a frenetic culmination as the river approaches, from above, the eastern rock wall of the Rift valley. This point may be reached by road from the south and one can stand on the actual rocky bank and observe the incredible spectacle offered by the maddened waters of the Nile, hurling themselves, not over a conventional rocky lip, but into a cleft scarcely 6 m wide (20 ft) to form the Murchison Falls. From there the waters drop for a tortuous 40 m (130 ft), before emerging into Baker's spume-flecked and crocodile-infested maelstrom, at the base of the cliff.

Looking to the west, the turbulent writhing waters grow quiescent. They spread out and soon seem almost lake-like. All the wild force and energy gone, replaced by an apparently purposeless and indolent meandering. This placidity will remain a characteristic of the next 4,827 km (3,000 miles) of the great river's course. Within 32 km (20 miles) of sultry luxuriance, the waters enter the northern reaches of Lake Albert: The Semliki and Victoria flows are now one. Finally, the waters of the Nile's many secret sources are joined, metamorphosing into the great mud-laden drain that the outside world calls the White Nile.

Below: Stanley and Livingstone at the mouth of the Rusizi River

Bibliography

Adams H G: 1890, *David Livingstone*, Hodder & Stoughton

Aeschylus: 525–456 BC; *Supplices 559*

Akeley, Mary L Jobe: 1931, *Carl Akeley's Africa*; Victor Gollanz

Alnaes, Kirsten: 1969, *Songs of the Rwenzururu Rebellion in Tradition & Transition in East Africa* (Ed P H Gulliver), Routledge & Kegan Paul

Amon Bazira: 1982, *Rwenzururu: 20 years of bitterness*; Origin not stated, 14 pp

Anderson, R M; May, R M & McLean, A R: 1988, *Possible demographic consequences of AIDS in developing countries*; *Nature*

Aristotle: 384-322 BC; *Meteorologica*, 1, 13

Baker, Samuel W: 1866, *The Albert Nyanza; Great Basin of the Nile*; Vols I & 2 Macmillan
: 1879, *Ismailia*, Macmillan

Baumann, O: 1894, *Durch Massailand zur Nilquelle: Reisen und Forschungen der Massai-Expedition des deutschen Antisklaverei-Komitee in den Jahren 1891–1893*, Berlin

Brown, L: 1971, *East African Mountains and Lakes*, East African Publishing House

Burton, Richard F: 1860, *The Lake Regions of Central Africa*; Longman, Green, Longman & Roberts (2 volumes)
:1872, *Zanzibar – City Island and Coast* (2 vols), Tinsley Bros
: 1894, *First Footsteps in East Africa* (2 vols), Tylsten & Edwards

Busk, Douglas: 1957, *The Fountains of the Sun*; Max Parrish

Claudius Ptolemaeus: 150 AD, *Geographia*, 1, 9 & 4, 8 (quoting Marinus of Tyre, *Periplus of the Erythrean Sea* 77 AD)

Cameron, V L: 1877, *Across Africa*, Vols I & II, Daldy Isbister

Carpenter, G D H: 1920, *A Naturalist on Lake Victoria*, Fisher Unwin

Casati, Gaetano: 1891, *Ten Years in Equatoria and the return with Emin Pasha*; Frederic Warne

Doornbos, Martin R: 1970, *Kumanyana and Rwenzururu: Two Responses to Ethnic Inequality in Protest and Power in Black Africa*, (Eds Robert I Rotberg & Ali M Mazrui, Oxford University Press, New York

Else, D: 1991, *Mountain Walking in Africa*, Robertson McCarta Ltd
: 1993, *Trekking in East Africa*, Lonely Planet Publications

Elton, J F. 1879, *Travels & Researches among the Lakes and Mountains of Eastern & Central Africa*, ed by Colterhill H. B, John Murray, reprinted 1968, Frank Cassolo

Farwell, Byron: 1963, *Burton*, Longmans

Fossey, Dian: 1983, *Gorillas in the Mist*, Houghton Mifflin, USA and Hodder & Stoughton, UK

Goldsmith, Edward: 1989, *Development: The Cause of the Population Explosion*, The Ecologist

Götzen, Graf A von: 1895, *Durch Afrika von Ost nach West*, Berlin

Grant, James Augustus: 1864, *A Walk across Africa, or Domestic Scenes from my Nile Journal*, William Blackwood

Hall, Richard: *Lovers on the Nile*, Collins

Herodotus: 486–408 BC, Book 2, *Euterpe 28*

Hurst, H E: 1927, *The Lake Plateau Basin of the Nile*, Cairo, Ministry of Public Works

Ingham, K: 1975, *The Kingdom of Toro in Uganda*, Studies in African History, Methuen

Jameson, J: 1890, *Story of the Rear Column*, R H Porter

Johnston, Harry H: 1902, *The Uganda Protectorate*, Hutchinson
1903, *The Nile Quest: a Record of the Exploration of the Nile and its Basin*; Lawrence & Bullen

Kandt, Richard: 1904, *Caput Nili: eine empfindsame Reise 3" der Quellen des Nils*; Dietrich Reimer (Ernst Vohfen), Berlin

Kafsir, Nelson: 1970, *Toro District: Society and Politics*, Mawazo
1976, *Ethnic Political Participation in Uganda: 3, Rwenzururu in the Shrinking Political Arena*, University of California Press, Berkeley & Los Angeles

Krapf, Johann Lewis: 1860, *Travels, Researches and Missionary Labours during an Eighteen Years' Residence in Eastern Africa*, Trubner (2nd edn Frank Cass, 1968)

Livingstone, David: 1857, *Missionary Travels and Researches in East Africa*, Harper
: 1899, *Livingstone's First Expedition to Africa*, Harper

Lugard, J P: 1893, *The Rise of our East African Empire*, William Blackwood

Maitland, A: 1973, *Speke*, Victorian and Modern history Book Club

Mason, A M: 1878, *Report of a Reconnaissance of Lake Albert made by order of His Excellency General Gordon Pasha, Governor-General of the Sudan*, Proceedings of the Royal Geographical Society

Moorehead, Alan: 1960, *The White Nile*, Hamish Hamilton

Mounteney, Jephson: 1890, *Emin Pasha – Rebellion at the Equator*, Sampson

Moyes, Barlett: 1956, *The King's African Rifles*, Gale & Polden

Ormerod W E: 1980-81, *The African Husbandsman and his Diseases: a moral dilemma posed by development versus ecological stability*, Rural Africana

Osmaston, H, Tukahirwa: 1996, Basalirwa, Nyakaana. *The Rwenzori Mountains National Park, Uganda*, Makerere University

Perham, Margery: 1956, *Lugard: The Years of Adventure 1858-1898*, Collins

Petherick, J: 1861, *Upper Egypt and Central Africa*, W Blackwood & Sons

Plath, D: 1996, *Uganda Rwenzori – A Range of Images*, Little Wolf Press

Robertson, J S: 1882, *Life of Livingstone*, Walter Scott

Robson, P: 1969, *Mountains of Kenya*, East African Publishing House

Royal Geographical Society, Notes by G E Crone: 1964, *The Sources of the Nile: Explorers' Maps AD 1856-1891*, Royal Geographical Society

Schaller, George: 1965, *The Year of the Gorilla*, Collins

Schlichter, Henry: 1891, *Ptolemy's Topography of Eastern Equatorial Africa*, Proceedings of the Royal Geographical Society

Schweinfurth, G: 1874, *Heart of Africa*, Harper

Shipton, Eric E: 1932, *Upon that Mountain*, Hodder & Stoughton

Speke, John Hanning: 1863, *Journal of the Discovery of the Source of the Nile*, William Blackwood
: 1864, *What led to the Discovery of the Source of the Nile*, Blackwood

Stacey, Tom: 1965, *Summons to Rwenzori*, Secker & Warburg

Stanley, Henry Morton: *How I found Livingstone; Travels, Adventures and Discoveries in Central Africa*, Sampson Low
1878, *Through the Dark Continent*, Sampson Low
1890, *In Darkest Africa; or TheQuest, Rescue and Retreat of Emin, Governor of Equatoria* (2 vols), Sampson Low

Stanley, Dorothy (ed):1914, *Autobiography of Henry M Stanley*, Sampson Low

Stanley, Richard & Nearne, Alan (eds): 1961, *The Exploration Diaries or H M Stanley*, William Kimber & Co

Stuhlmann, Franz: 1894, *Mit Emin Pascha ins Herz von Afrika*, Reimer, Berlin

Tanzania: Crisis & Struggle for Survival: 1986, Eds J Boesen, Kjell K Havenik, Juhani Koponen, Rie Odgaard; Scandinavian Institute for African Studies, Upsala, Sweden

Synge, P M: 1937, *Mountains of the Moon*, reprinted 1985, Waterstone & Co

Taylor, B K: 1962, *The Western Lacustrine Bantu: the Konjo*, International African Institute, London

Thomson, J: 1881, *To the Central Lakes and Back*, (2 vols), Sampson Low
: 1885, *Through Masai Land*, Sampson Low

Tilman, H W: 1937, *Snow on the Equator*; Bell

Uganda-Congo Boundary Commission: 1910, *Agreement between Great Britain and Belgium settling the boundary between Great Britain and the Congo*, Brussels, May 14th 1910, British & Foreign State Papers

Uganda Now: Between Decay and Development: 1988, Eds Hölger Bernt Hansen and Michael Twaddle, East African Studies; J Currie, London and Heinemann, Nairobi

Uganda Government: 1962, *Report of the Commission of Inquiry into the Recent Disturbances amongst the Baamba and Bakonjo People of Toro*, Government Printer, Entebe, Uganda

Waller: 1874, *Last Journals of Livingstone*, Murray

Wielochowski, A: 1986, *East Africa International Mountain Guide*, West Col Productions

Wood, Michael: 1987, *Different Drums*, Century

Yeoman, G: 1989, *Africa's Mountains of the Moon: Journeys to the Snowy Sources of the Nile*, Hamish Hamilton, London

Yeoman, G & Walker, J: 1967, *The Ixodid Ticks of Tanzania*

Above: *The village potter at work*

Index